Successful
Management
Styles of
India

VOL
1

I0490462

WHAT IS DIFFERENT IS

RAJASEKHAR
POLAPRAGADA

INDIA · SINGAPORE · MALAYSIA

Notion Press

Old No. 38, New No. 6
McNichols Road, Chetpet
Chennai - 600 031

First Published by Notion Press 2020
Copyright © Rajasekhar Polapragada 2020
All Rights Reserved.

ISBN

Hardcase: 978-1-64869-905-4
Paperback: 978-1-64850-874-5

Dedicated to my guru

Sri Satya Sai Baba

who taught us

"Education without character and
Business without ethics are dangerous to society"
23 November 2019

Hyderabad – India

CONTENTS

WHY DID I WRITE THIS BOOK?

In 2008, when I was the Vice President of a mega project in India, I used to report to Gordon, who was our project director. We used to meet at breakfast table in our guest house and discuss the progress of the project. Invariably, *Gordon* would come to a phrase called "Indian management". I used to argue, while the principles of management are same all over the world, practice may be different, based on our culture and traditions. When I started observing successful managers around me, I found some are street smart, some are strugglers and some did exceptionally well. I understood that these changes are personal traits incorporated by leaders to achieve success. Management and Leadership are interchangeable words as per Peter Drucker and what works well changes with people and situation. As my thoughts started crystalizing, my project was complete and I observed it is different from known financial and management principles. You may call it "Jugad" or Indian management style. Then I thought of sharing my experience of "what works in India, what does not work". Like in any other country, Indians also approve some practices and dislike or disapprove certain leadership styles thus influencing the "3M"s Men, Money and Management.

What Indians to do well is summed-up by highly innovative skill called *"jugad"* and adaptability to conditions necessitated and sharpened by tolerance and patience learnt from lack of resources from a millennium of foreign rule. If Indian corporations get into the habit of continuous improvement, and adopt best practices of others, they can be role models for the world. The main thrust of the book is author's recommendation to Business leaders to focus on 2 policies and 4 principles to transform India into an economic super power.

As I started writing this book, it expanded into Tri series, which was beyond my control. I explained in this first volume "what is different in Indian Management." Other two volumes cover "How to be the best " and "Beyond sustainability?" I included some slides which sum up the points for the benefit of students and easy summing for executives. Further research is required on "Ancient Indian Management styles" which I believe will benefit *Indian economy as well as world in achieving sustainability.*

This book is written mainly for young graduates fresh from business schools, who find real situations different from what they studied in books. Also those who want to invest in India may find some useful hints in this book to be successful in India

It is my gut feeling that if you are successful in India, you can be successful in any part of the world. I consider my effort successful, if readers, observe some of the Indian traits mentioned in the book and get "De ja Vous ......" feelings when they face similar situations.

Enjoy the book "Successful management Styles of India - Volume 1"

(What is different?)
Rajasekhar Polapragada Dt 14 July 2019
MD- Economic Engineering Excellence. Portland-USA
email: pbrajasekhar@gmail.com
Twitter and Face-book "Raj Polapragada"
www.EconomicEngineeringExcellence.org
Sarve jana sukhino bhavantu!
(Let all Prosper!)

23, November 20019

Hyderabad

ACKNOWLEDGMENT

First and foremost, I would like to thank our ancient Indian rishis and wisemen, who are responsible for the traditions of this great country based on which our Temple management runs even to-day. Next, I want to thank my father Sri Polapragada Satyanarayana murthy, for teaching me, success of any person is not achieving greatness, but in developing a competent successor. I am thankful to my mother, Smt Polapragada Rajya Lakshmi who taught me relations are more important than results.

My special thanks to my brother Shri PLN Murthy, my friends Hariharan Mahadevan, Manepalli Venkata SivaPrasad and Shri Kishor Makadia, who acted as sound boards for formulating my thoughts to write this book........ I thank all my ex-colleagues in India and abroad who taught me something or other in managing situations.

This acknowledgement will not be complete without thanking Prof V. Raghunathan, author of "Games Indians play". I was inspired by numerous western management experts to write this book which is based on my own study.

Finally, I thank my wife Smt. Polapragada Lakshmi Sekhar, who challenged me with her contrasting management style and proved Indian management style works well in many situations.

Rajasekhar Polapragada

PART I

HISTORY AND TRADTION OF INDIA

"we owe a lot to Indians who taught the world how to count, by inventing zero"

– Albert Einstein

1

INDIA'S LONG HISTORY AND LEADERSHIP

> *"Centuries to come, people can hardly believe,*
> *Mahatma Gandhi like person walked on this planet"*
>
> *— Albert Einstein*

It was a winter morning 7 AM. The place was the guest house of a large Business house in western India. Sun was just rising in the sky filling the golden light all around the swimming pool and club house. It had become a morning routine for both of us to meet at break-fast table and discuss the USD 2 Billion mega project early in the morning. I was the head of the process while Gordon was the project director. Looking into the space between the green grass and the blue sky, Gordon asked me, "Raj, can you imagine, any good reason why the person who recruited me as Director-projects wants to create hurdles in my work?" Remembering his earlier remarks, I was quick to respond "you mean, Indian Management?" Gordon quickly changed his tone and said "No! I am not complaining about management style. Don't you think, my failure is my boss's failure?", With a tone of reconciliation, I asked Gordon "do you mean back-seat driving? or just not letting you take decisions?" "If it is latter", I continued, "do not bother about it "Empowerment" does not exist in the dictionary of many Indian Leaders. "is Empowerment not preferred in India? or is it Micro management? ",Gordon continued his query. I cleared my throat and started my long explanation," many successful leaders In India think, no system works in India without personal touch. So they developed their own unique way of achieving success. Unless you fall in line, they will not be convinced that you can achieve success. You may call it lack of confidence but based on their past experience, they do not want you to try and fail. Many successful managers feel, no system works in the absence of team spirit and unity. "Empowerment" is possible after you are acceptable. If we look at ancient India, Leaders were near perfect or demi-gods. When public start accepting their leaders, then every thing would fall in place. To explain general acceptability, I started introducing Gordon to ancient Indian leadership. Thus started my one year long association with Gordon, which culminated in writing this Tri volume series book, "Successful Management Style of India."

1.1 LEADERS OF ANCIENT INDIA

Gordon wanted to know "why acceptability of a leader is very important in India. I told him "When a leader is accepted by all stake holders, the Leader may automatically become powerful. Indians are emotional and highly loyal to their leaders as well as their companies, India has a long history of leaders with different Leadership styles. But few like Sri Ram are accepted by all. Sriram is the hero of Ramayana, which is very popular even in remote villages of India, since thousands of years. Mahabharata, an epic whose hero was Sri Krishna, dates back to 5030 BC. Buddha who influenced millions of people even in China, Thailand, and far off Japan, walked on this land 2000 years back. Sriram, Sri Krishna and Buddha are 3 great leaders of ancient India, among dozens of great leaders, who influenced Indian thinking and culture.

Sri Ram went to forest abdicating his throne for 14 years to fulfill his father's promise. India has a long tradition of children who obey their parents and have general respect for elders and bosses. Ironically, Spirit of Freedom runs high in India, which may be attributed to a unique feature of Hinduism to worship a deity of your choice. However, obeying elders and loyalty are reserved for the leaders who are accepted and respected. Following traditions runs in the veins of Indians, while rebels are given freedom to question and the choice of following their own faith. So dissent is not favored but tolerated in India which is unique feature in Indian culture. Krishna was a master trouble shooter and a strategist par excellence who advised even Rajas and Maharajas.

Buddha followed principles of non violence and emphasized wisdom and right path which influenced kings and poor alike. Many changed their warring life style and adopted non-violence. I quickly clarified to Gordon, that present leaders need not be like the ancient Indian Leaders. In India, empowerment and succession are not easy to achieve, unless a leader performs near miracles or achieves impossible. Thus, the day started with ancient Indian leadership and continued for few days and finally Indian management remained an enigma to Gordon and a puzzle for me to explain.

Leadership Styles – Ancient India

While India has history of thousands of years, three great personalities dominated ancient India, kings Sri Rama , Sri Krishna and Siddharth (later became Buddha) alone swayed millions of people in India and abroad with their universal acceptance .

source: Successful Management styles of India

As any Indian would tell you, leadership skills of Sriram were phenomenal as he led an army of monkeys who had no discipline. Krishna was an accepted leader by all the kings of India during His time, though he did not rule any kingdom. Coming to Buddha, he changed the course of several rulers of India, paving way for Buddhism not only in India but also as far as China and Japan in the East.

Leadership styles of Ancient India

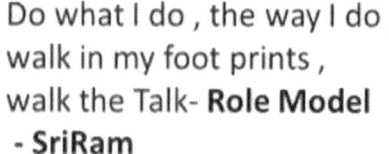

Do what I do , the way I do ,
walk in my foot prints ,
walk the Talk- **Role Model**
- SriRam

Do what I say,
follow my directions,
Follow God , fight the Evil ! **- Director**
-SriKrishna

Think the way I think,
Follow the Righteous Path – **Leader**
- Buddha

source: Successful Management styles of India

Gordon wondered, if he has to reach the heights of Sri Ram or, Sri Krishna or Buddha. I assured Gordon, it is not necessary though if he reaches the heights of ancient Indian leaders, it would be great. But in general, Indians expect their leaders to be larger than real life and expect they forgive their staff for their weakness and short comings. But empowerment and succession are not easy to achieve as acceptability is a bigger criterion than achievement and qualification. Then our discussion spilled to present times and more recent Leaders of India.

1.2 LEADERS OF INDIA BEFORE INDPENDENCE

The next day, I began my discourse on Indian Leadership and explained that India and China were the wealthiest nations till as late as 17th Century which were quoted in ancient Egypt, Persian, Greek and Roman history books.

Indian Leadership Styles – Before Independence

Chanakya established Mighty Maurya Kingdom which stalled Alexander the great, enter India . Though many Muslim kings ruled India for over a millennium, Akbar the Great alone won the hearts of Hindus and Muslims alike. Shivaji, the great Martha warrior is head and shoulders above others whom India recognised for fighting with Moghuls and rallied all Indians against foreign rule.

The Leadership style depends on the place and situation. Chanakya had to bring about a sort of revolution from a lethargic, corrupt rule to a dynamic system with social awakening, For centuries, Chanakya became a role model for rulers and public alike. Of the Moghul dynasty, Akbar alone brought about social peace and co-existence among two religions Hindus and Muslims. Shivaji inculcated confidence and courage in public, so that they could fight the formidable opponents. Each had a path, principle and goal.

Indian Leaders before Independence

Never Trust the Enemy ,
Use your own Wisdom
- **Role Model for Starategy**
- **Chankaya**

Make friends with Enemy
Freedom of Religion
- **Benevolent Dictator**
- **Akbar the Great**

Courage is required to fight formidable Enemy
Unity of Indians ,
Valor and strategy – **Leader**
- **Shivaji**

As India was under foreign rule till 1947, Leaders prior to independence were those who united India or tried to liberate India.

Some of them were social reformers and some of them were spiritual leaders. *Vinoba Bhave* led the *"Bhudan Movement"* (collecting land from rich peacefully and distributing to poor). These leaders helped Indian renaissance which kept the nation revived from hundreds of years of Muslim invasions and savage. By convincing rich to give up their of land, *Viniba Bhave* helped India to skip the revolutions similar to what happened in France and Russia by bringing rich and poor on the same platform. Leaders like *Bipin Chandra Pal, Chitta Ranjan Das* helped the nation to give a new thrust to modern education. Aravind Ghosh revived ancient spiritual wisdom after a stint with freedom struggle condemning colonial rule. *Vivekanada* is an icon of youth kindling courage and self respect. He had awakened Indian youth and was the first to arrive at Chicago to win the hearts of America, long before Gandhi swept the world leaders with his non-violence. *Raja Ram Manohar Roy* helped Indians get rid of superstitions and dogma by introducing widow marriages and educating women. The Indian Renaissance has taken place simultaneously while freedom struggle was going on. Each of these leaders had mass following and some are more popular than national leaders, Gandhi and Nehru. The media being under control of British, has not done justice to not recording many achievements of these leaders.

Indian Renaissance

Raja Ram Mohan Roy

Desh Bandhu Chittaranjan Das

source: Successful Management styles of India

Each of these Leaders had their own management style, Some of them were benevolent dictators, some were wise preachers. But all of them influenced Indian thought and the style of leadership in managing the problems. Thus Indian management style has been "top to bottom" than "bottom to top". I explained to Gordon, it is difficult for many leaders to be in the shoes of Gandhi. Gandhi, achieved a cult status not only in India but also all-over the world**.**

1.3 LEADERS OF INDPEDENCE STRUGGLE

Political leaders like Gandhi, Patel and Nehru figure high in the list of people who exhibited management styles which are similar except Netaji Subhash Chandra Bose who lead an army against British and influenced rural and educated people. Contrary to the British history books, it is the revolt of Navy in Mumbai in 1946 after world war II, which prompted Atlee, then PM of UK, to hasten declaring independence to India.

Indian Leaders – National /Political Leaders

Subhash Chandra Bose
ସୁଭାଷ ଚନ୍ଦ୍ର ବୋଷ
(23rd January, 1897 - 18th August, 1945)

While many figure out in this list such as Balagangadhar Tilak ,father of modern Independent struggle, who invited Gandhi to take over the mantle of Leadership and Sardar Patel who integrated 300 odd small kingdoms into Indian republic. All those leaders fall into two categories based on their principle of struggle, namely, Non- violence and   Direct action.

Each of these leaders like Shri Ram, Sri Krishna, Buddha, Chanakya, Akbar, Shivaji, Gandhi, Nehru and Patel deserve separate research projects to study their leadership styles and understand how Indian public responded to them. Particularly, Gandhi inspired friends and foes alike. Those who were close like Khan Abdul Gaffer khan of Afghanistan, known as Border Gandhi or people far from America, like Albert Einstein praised him alike. Centuries to come, humanity will have difficulty in believing a person like Gandhi walked on this planet with principles of Non-Violence and Truth. Gordon was curious to know how Gandhi was inspired to follow Non-Violence. I explained non-violence is not new to India as Buddha walked on this land 2000 years back converting almost all the kings to Buddhism and non-violence. Ashoka the great had commanded kingdom spreading from Sri Lanka to Kazakhstan. Buddhism spread to China, Far-East and Japan. Some management systems like Temple Management existed not just since centuries, but millennium, dating to much before Buddha and Mahavir. You can find Hindu temples in as far as Cambodia.

Gordon appreciated that ancient leaders as well as recent leaders stuck to democracy and secularism. I explained that Hindu religion which had freedom to worship, accepted even atheists as part of them, leave alone who got independence accepting other religions. As a result even before Christ, India had many religions like Buddhism, Jainism and Indians gave asylum to Jews, persecuted Parsees from Iran and even Syrian Christians. The largest democracy gave voting rights to women and one of the first few countries to elect female leaders. One can not ignore that United States of America took a century to give vote to Blacks and get them out of slavery. That was the vision of our elders as well as a task for us to bring all Indians on to a single mind. Pluralism is the back bone of India and democracy is the only way to manage. Secularism is an important tenet of Hinduism. Slowly our discussion moved to the traditional management methods of India. I explained to Gordon that ancient India had several management techniques though many are extinct, some of the old Indian systems which function even to-day are

1.   Temple Management

2. Indian wedding *(shadi)* management

3. Festival or *mela* (Indian fair) management.

1.4 LEADERS IN SCIENCE, ENGINEERING AND BUSINESS

In the modern education of science and engineering also India produced leaders; some received Noble prizes and few migrated to developed nations to continue their research and became famous. Sir **CV Raman** received Nobel prize in Physics and **Bose** of Bose-Einstein theory and many more great personalities are not covered in this book due to lack of space and relevance. They are all leaders in their own way. But two fields, Atomic and Space research need special mention as the achievements are phenomenal. They achieved great feats at moderate costs with meagre help from western advanced research facilities.

Indian Leaders– Scientists and Engineers

M. Viswesarayya   Sir C.V. Raman   H.J.Baba   Vikram Sarabai

MokshaGundam Viswesarayya was an Engineer who guided Mysore Maharaja , Nijam . CV Raman was a Noble laurates in Physics . Homi Jahangir Bhaba is father of the Indian Nuclear Engineering while Vikram Sarabhai is father Indian space research , which made Indian Engineers and Scientists world famous.

In the field of Business and Industry, many names come up, but some names who revolutionized the India business model are mentioned here.

Indian Leaders– Entrepreneurs

JRD Tata and now his heir Ratan Tata set the tone foe Ideal MNC in India. GD Birla who has supported Gandhi has so many family members who are successful and thus TATA , Birla became familiar names in Indian household . As each businessman is different, centuries old trade is what has made Indian known to the world and its riches had in fact prompted invaders to conquer India. Thus it is imperative to know the unique Leadership and Management style of India

www.helpyoursociety.in   source: Successful Management styles of India   ©ABCD of Leadership

1.5 DIFFERENT LEADERSHIP STYLES

Management is tough in India during festivals with large crowds. A glaring example is Traffic Management which many attribute to lack of discipline and some to lack of infrastructure facilities. "Successful Management styles of India were based on traditional Management techniques like Temple Management and Mela (Fair) or Festive management as it is traditionally done in India. However, majority management principles are based on western management such as Administration, control, and staffing, where a Leader can show the difference is in people Management and sharing of Vision and inspiring staff.

1.5.1 ACCEPTABILITY

As Leadership style might vary with the leader, public expectation is high since India produced leaders like Mahatma (great soul) Gandhi, who are still kept at a high pedestal by world leaders and intellectuals.

What are you ?

- what value we add to this world,

- whose footsteps we followed to reach here and

- What foot prints we leave behind for others to follow

Will decide

- if we are a legend or
- If you are at a dead end !

© ABCD of Leadership

Leadership styles

- Leaders are of different styles.
- Some lead from the front, while others guard from behind .
- Some communicate, while others listen and understand.
- Some are transparent and others inspire trust.
- Some are brilliant ,while others are wise by being silent.
- Some are courageous, while others protect their followers from all dangers.
- But situations create leaders, while leaders do not create situations.
- What Gandhi did in 1947, He may not be able to repeat to-day.
- What worked yesterday, may not work to-day.
- What worked for you, may not work for me.
- That is why I say, Leadership is situational and result oriented.
- What works is leadership and
- what is right has to be followed, even if does not work.
- That is the value based leadership.
-
- **We have to be different from others to be a leader.**
- **But we have to right , to be a respected leader.**

copyright helpyoursocietyally.aboo.com

In short, Acceptability became the main criterion for any leader and without it, it is difficult to perform at his/her best. Thus historically, the foundation of Successful Management style of India became ACCEPTABILITY. Loyalty of team members depend on Acceptability. Thus both have become so intertwined, Leaders who accept weaknesses and failure of team members are liked by many followers.

2

TRADITIONAL INDIAN MANAGEMENT TECHNIQUES

"There is no book so thrilling, educative and authoritative than Upanishads"

– Max Muller

CELEBRATION IS TO INVOLVE ALL

After a week, during our evening tea, Gordon wondered why every milestone of the project is celebrated with so much fan-fare. At the function of laying foundation stone of our administration building, each team member had to break the coconut as an auspicious gesture. Gordon referred to that ceremony, which went on for few hours till lunch. I explained, that is the way, we celebrate festivals in India to involve all members. There is no special Employee engagement. All festivals involve other communities also. For example *Holi* is not essentially a Hindu festival. *Onam* festival is celebrated by all religions in Kerala. Many in UP celebrate *Ram Lila*. These festivals, are great source of unity where rich and poor, ruling class and commoners rub their shoulders and celebrate. These festivals were well utilized by father of Indian freedom movement *Balagangadhar Tilak* to rekindle freedom movement. Some of the festivals like Holi are celebrated by Hindus and Muslims together. Gordon said, he started liking Indian festivals which are celebrated with enthusiasm and fervor, as they strengthened relations among people. I explained to Gordon, further advantages of celebrating these festivals. In fact, these festivals are source of fun and many look forward to them as they provide good relaxation for people who are tired of problems and stress of work.

These festivals have helped Indian society to be close knit than develop as group of individuals. Festivals helped Indians to develop collective consciousness. Festivals, functions, *melas* (large gathering similar to a fair in an English village), Religious congregations like ***Kumbha mela*** (a religious festival that is celebrated four times over the course of 12 years, on the banks of river Ganga) are attended by many without fail. For Indians these are very important part of life!

For centuries, Indians used many methods, techniques to manage and administer Temples, festivals, weddings etc. mastering Team building. Education and Health management and even village administration existed till Muslim invasions restricted them. Later during British rule many new systems were introduced and some old traditions became extinct. Another interesting phenomenon, unique to India is Vocational and employment systems. They created a social balance which were later maligned by caste disputes in later years during British regime. Vocation and family profession system are unique, which need a separate study, Research and understanding. What is unique about this vocational system? Unemployment was zero which is still a less understood phenomenon. Gordon wanted to know more about these systems, which I said, it calls for experts, not a mortal being like me to comment on a thousand year old tradition. But I promised to explain system which are still existing and followed by many Indians.

Some of the old Indian systems functioning since the past several centuries which still exist to-day are:

1. **Temple Management:** Temples which acted as cultural hubs, Economic centers, where Education, vocational training is imparted and arts flourished. Indian Society evolved and revolved around temples.

2. **Indian wedding (*shadi is a Hindi word for wedding*) management:** which brings, friends, relatives and whole villages together and for centuries inculcated comradeship and cooperation.

3. **Festival or *mela* (Indian fair) management.** which achieved the impossible of combining discipline and devotion among general public, without any external pressure or force.

4. Application of Modern management principles is tough in India. Two glaring examples are Traffic Management and Time Management. Some may attribute the failure of these systems to lack of discipline among crowds and large numbers, far exceeding capability of administration control. Traffic management, at best, can be compared to disaster management during natural calamities. In situations such as forest fire, flood situation or Hurricane in USA, damage control is the priority. Of course every Indian has his own theory to explain the traffic problem, ranging from mistaken definition of freedom to lack of resources. Traffic and Time Management are covered in detail in the next chapter.

2.1 TEMPLE MANAGEMENT

Till 1000 AD, virtually world market and trade was monopolized by India and China. The enormous wealth, which Indian temples were handling was the main attraction for the Muslim invaders such as **Mohammad Ghori** and **Ghajani.** Many temples like **Somnath** temple in Gujarat and other temples in northern India were looted or stripped off assets. South Indian temples were spared a little by powerful kingdoms, of *Viajayanagar* and *Maratha* empires. Later in 19ᵗʰ century, management of richest temples such as Tirupati temple were taken-over by British empire. Since ages, Indian temples were centers of culture, education, crafts, arts and even had *khazana* (wealth) of the kings, Libraries and many more features like application of crafts. It is worth knowing that many temples were bigger than to-day's largest banks as India was richest Country which attracted Greek, British and Islamic countries alike.

Unique features of temple management

In spite of having different ownership, Temple management has some common features.

- NO visible management, but mostly run by traditions.

- No single chain of command (Multi-chain of command)

- No Accountability, but full responsibility!

- Preference to oral Communication and command

- Freedom to devotees within the umbrella of sanctity.

- Finance centres with world's oldest Banking system.

- Knowledge Centres of Arts and Science.

- Voluntary contribution of funds.

- Traditional based and not Rule based management

Temple management is acceptable to all the stake holders as they follow Traditions which are accepted norms. This aspect collective consciousness is secret of success of many Business Enterprises in India.

- Best part of temple management which is liked by many is "No work and no responsibility is given for visitors." This may be one reason **for general lack of responsibility in public domain in India.** Gordon gave a look of appreciation as if he found a reason for the lack of responsibility, which is one of his complaints.

- Temple Management is **Acceptable** to all as per Indian Tradition which later became a pre-requisite for Leaders. A question often asked by bosses is "what was our earlier practice?

- One can visit a Temple of his choice, which is basic foundation on which Hindu religion is built. This sense of **Freedom is reflected in many walks of life in India.** As it is different from monistic religions and Temples flourished in India and Temples encouraged plural society since ages.

- **No compulsion to donate** to the Temple-fund. Thus participation without commitment is accepted in India society.

- However It is Obligatory for all to follow personal Hygiene and sanctity of the Temple.

Though most of the temples follow some discipline, it is mainly voluntary to follow discipline. It is limited to maintain the sanctity, but not necessarily to keep order, queues and recommendations. One of the unique features of temple management is acceptance of tradition and **karma** theory (wrongly equated to fatalism by west) which makes management easy in India to the extent of accepting rules, though may not be affective implementing discipline.

Temple Management – why Acceptable ?

- Indian tradition is not to question, but to obey.
- Mostly free and no compulsory contributions.
- Many charitable acts like poor feeding are associated with it.
- Resources are not the concern of general public
- No accountability
- Can participate if interested(voluntary work)
- No responsibility
- Engagement and entertainment as many temples are centres of arts.

Multi chain of command and Acceptability are two main features of Temple management as it is a traditional method accepted by Indian public for centuries.

Temple Management Uniqueness - Multi chain of command (MCC)

- Multi Chain of command is Unique feature of Temple Management .
- Single chain of command is suitable only for small enterprises.
- Some examples of public domains dotted with MCC
  (Multi Chain of Command)
  Eg. Festivals and Pilgrim places , Indian Temples
- Enforcing discipline is difficult in single chain of command as communication takes time to suit dynamic situations.

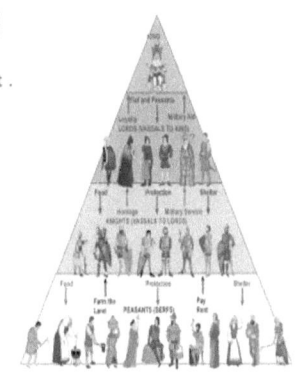

Systems and Procedures: The plot, plan of a Temple represents the cosmos and there is a separate procedure explained in *"Agama sastra"* (age old tradition stipulated by sages) which explains how to build a temple and run the temples, which is followed even today. Some of the features adopted from Temple management by successful Indian Managers are keeping the Enterprise as a Loyal group who voluntarily work for temple, make it benevolent and welfare oriented. Thus systems and procedures used in Temple management are thousands of years old and all are well documented, which is unique feature of Temple Management. That is the reason even though many temples were destroyed during 1000 years of foreign rule, new temples or re-constructed temples had no problem in establishing themselves. In spite of a common code of conduct, each temple has its own unique tradition which has local, cultural and historical origins.

Multi-chain of Command

Temples have Multi–chain of command. One chain of command looks after Administration called *"Dharma Karta"* represented by King or his representative. Other group called *Archakas* or *Pujaris* (priests) who carry out devotional activities. Third is headed by elders in the village which is a big group taking care of all literary, arts and other activities including the discipline and behavior of the crowd. Multi hierarchy has its own strengths and weakness, but it is the only working method in large groups where freedom and devotion are the hall-marks.

However, Multi-chain of common can be also every one pulling in different directions. While on major issues, a consensus exists in Temples, there are so many minor issues which lead to murmurs. Multi-Chain of command can lead to a storm, if vested interests are at play and divisive forces will have advantage. It is not uncommon to find back-seat driving in multi-chain of command. Inspite of all this, Temples are working well as expectations are less general commitment of devotees is more.

If the involved parties in Multi-management are compatible, it will be a smooth sail or it will rock the boat. *Unity and consensus are essential in Multi*

Management style and if any thing short of 100% alignment, it shows up in the *management.* That is why traditions, respect for elders and Transparency are essential in Temple Management. **Acceptability, Tolerance, Patience and Non – Violence are the elements contributing to Peaceful operation of temples.** Temple Management needs a separate study as it has the potential to bring back Indian Economy to its past glory.

Multiple chain of Command gives multiple choices to work

2.2.1.1 INDIAN WEDDING MODEL

Gordon had a good occasion to attend wedding of our owner's daughter. it was performed on the lawns of posh Mahalakshmi race course club in Mumbai, in a grand manner fit for a wedding of Maharaja. Gordon marveled at the arrangements and was surprised by the huge amount spent for wedding. After the wedding, Gordon asked me, "is it necessary to invite so many guests and does it justify the cost as many did not even meet the bride and bridegroom after the dinner." I explained to Gordon, in India, wedding is a life time project. Both celebrating a wedding and Building a house are considered big projects in India. Not only both involve huge amount of spending and sometimes more than life time's earnings of many Indians. There is a saying in our language, a man is considered successful in his life, only after building a house and perform a wedding. These are considered an achievements in one's life, as not only cost, but arranging resources, managing the multiple problems of family and society.

In many developed countries, people buy a house early in their life, with the help of loans; Where as in India, it is a life long goal and at the time of retirement, they build a house as per their financial ability. So also, a wedding of their children is performed with savings of a life time. Though marriage is for two adults, the whole family, not only from both sides of bride and bride groom, but all near and dear attend the wedding and but participate in every event of wedding. The cost is enormous. Relatives and friends think, if they do not attend the wedding, it is disrespect to the parents of bride and bride groom.

Team spirit at it's peak

Now let us see how a wedding is conducted and what is the role of visitors in the wedding. If any one is thinking it is performed by one and others watch it, they have not understood India. It is like a festival, participated by all. The welcome dance called *"barat"* is an occasion for all to participate and dance, to express their happiness, show solidarity and Team spirit. There will be one or the other activity, each will do and that is best of engaging guests. If we apply, management principles it is like all employees are engaged in an on going Project or plan. It is a case of collective responsibility and engaging all the participants and working in harmony with a single objective of success and building the Team all together in one act.

Budget beyond estimate

Indian Wedding is a unique affair where most of the of the participants spend money beyond their means. It is not just cost alone, the scale and manner in which a wedding is performed in India is worth studying further as a management model. There are several middle class families who spend half of their life's earning for the weddings and few take loans which some times alter their life style and make them poor. The cost apart, the way, near and dear join the wedding and help the family is a big subject on which a family concept and its importance are dependent. Though like Temple Management, Indian wedding may not call for huge funds for research, Mela and Festivals which runs into millions of total expenditure is worth studying. There was an un-official estimate that Kumbha Mela in UP state costs around USD 1 Billion of public spending, not counting many times the cost by private funding.

Trouble with Indian economy is that most of their money is locked in assets such as Gold and real estate. Gold reserves with individuals in India are estimated to be highest in the world. Long foreign rule and nuncertain economy and security reasons promoted amny Indians to par their funds in Gold and land. Hence spending beyond budget results in liquidation of assets in many cases. It Is mind boggling to compare cost of Wedding, Festivals, Temples assets, expenditure including private, public and society cannot be explained with low GDP of India. Many attribute it to parallel economy or Black money. This is one of the factors which hinder Transparency in India. Finances of Political parties, temple managements and few individuals are not documented properly. Some have foreign assets and some hide in charitable institutions. But a Big fat wedding is an enigma in India.

2.3 FESTIVAL-*MELA* (FAIR) MODEL

It is common observation in Mumbai, the capital of Maharashtra state in India, virtually city stands still for 11 days during **Ganapati Puja.** Until the time idol is immersed in the sea, office attendance is thin, schools close down and crowds throng streets at Ganesh festival pandals (here puja is performed). Often road are partially blocked. Similarly in Calcutta and Gujarat Navaratri festival I performed with fervor, and so is *Ramlila* is performed Delhi. Festivals in India are a passion like Cricket and Bollywood (an acronym for Hindi Cinema)....... During thee festivals and *mela* (village fair) like kumbha mela, there is no single location for celebration, but whole place, city or river Ganga becomes the arena for celebration. People from all over the country, visit and participate. some visitors come individually, some in groups and there is no limit for number groups and the population looks like ocean.

In Indian corporate offices also, one can see Christmas like celebration for Deepavali (festival of lights). If you observe how management principles are applied during this period, it is amazing as these are not planned as much as we expect them to be. Though one cannot say planning is absent it does not show up or is dynamic as flow of humanity changes. Same way discipline is not imposed, but celebration finds its own way of flow and it is easier to experience than explain. So I chose to highlight this unique Indian way of managing to Gordon. Gordon was simply astonished at the enormity of size and scale.

A group of management students studied Kumbh Mela, which is largest congregation of human convergence, estimated to be 100 million pilgrims, had a record of least number of loss of human lives and accidents. The findings are interesting as devotion dictated the discipline than governance of crowds by local authorities.

Tradition takes over Management

During Festivals and Fairs (Mela), it is a case of Tradition over-ruling management and control unlike in the west, where it is a strict discipline model. As a popular Russian catch phrase (during height of communism) "Big-brother is watching", tradition is the watch dog in India. Only difference is that no body can point out a group of people or leaders, who are in control of the situation. Indians are different in that sense like Japanese are different, where unions behave differently to express their resentment and over produce the goods to create a glut in the market. *In India, if the individuals are silent, we need to understand, they are showing their disapproval.* In festivals, tradition takes over and individuals will have less say and less control on the events. There may be few unruly groups, but *overall, tradition and faith are in control of the events.* Nothing is visible, except faith and tradition. You may call it blind faith or total surrender. It is not easy to explain to an outsider as change, takes place, it takes place slowly. But no force and no rigid discipline is visible.

Who is in control?

We often wonder who is managing the show in festivals and, *melas?* It is a million dollar question! I recall one funny incident happened, during our college days, when we visited a Petroleum refinery in south India. As students, we were wonder struck by seeing a modern automatic petroleum refinery Fluidized catalytic cracking unit (FCC) which converts heavy petroleum fractions to Gasoline. The sheer size with a height of a multi story building of over 150 feet height with lift to reach top of the regenerator, over whelmed us. Once or twice an operator had to go to the top of the unit and collect samples. We started bombarding the foreman with a lot of questions. At one time, foreman was fed up with our silly questions. He was a science graduate and could not answer few questions related to Engineering design. He was not an engineer, but reached that position by sheer dedication, hard work and of course operational experience. He took us out of the control room into the open air and looked at sky and said" it is run by God's grace". If *Melas* and festivals are managed like that which I call *"discreet Management", where enthusiasm inspires discipline.*

Some times, no-body manages or it appears to be so. What works in temple management is applicable in Wedding and Festival Model also. All three are supported by Indian culture and survived for centuries. However, for those who want to apply proven management principles, multi tasking and multi-management is the biggest problem. The task is to keep the common values and ethics in tact which is possible only by if men at helm of affairs acts as role model.

Multi-tasking and Multiple Hierarchy

It may not be possible for all CEOs to do Multi-tasking. It is as risky as mountaineering and few are willing to take the risk. Where as, multi -management is akin to back seat driving which is done by owners in private companies and government bureaucrats in Public sector companies. *This poses a peculiar problem with an opportunity for personal style of management in India*. Some organizations related to defense ministry like Atomic commission and Space agency have flourished with strict meritorious hierarchy with Government patronage. But majority of Enterprises were not successful like Banking sector, where individual management styles did not work and many ran into problem of Non performing Assets. In most companies, press and public interfere and without knowledge of economics and Management, public give their views and some times factories are forced to close not by environment but for political reasons. These are the hard realities, though rare, one needs caution in dealing with these back seat drivers. *In fact, Public Sector units had this peculiar priority to keep the jobs of employees at the cost of viability of the company.*

Some times, multi tasking, some times multi-management, once in a while, back seat driving, may look crazy. But what works is the technique for which many do not have a standard practice. *It is like a parachute diving, a qualified person can land properly while inexperienced people land in bushes.*

Herculean Task to build Teams

To explain the difficulty of any task, let us look at one small episode in Ramayana, the oldest recorded book or history in the world. Sri Ram was a king of *Ayodhya* who had to cross the ocean to reach Sri Lanka to rescue his queen. The toughest part of battle was crossing the ocean. His army was thousands of monkeys. One can imagine the patience required to keep discipline of an army consisting of monkeys. Each team member expects his leader to have as much patience of

Sri Ram to forgive team's faults and mistakes, train them, develop them. Though Gordon never questioned me, I guess, he must have realized acceptability has nothing to do with Empowerment or Leadership. Indian traditional way of temple management and festival management has some useful lessons for project management such as building a bridge across ocean by the monkey army using floating rocks. It is a herculean task if not impossible.

Indian traditional management styles may not be always working in modern times, but the underlying principle of general acceptance and top down management style and expecting an extremely capable, patient, benevolent leader is still an expectations in India which can be seen in Indian Enterprises like in Indian films.

In short, The Leaders are expected to be Heroes, Charismatic, with larger than life image, Capable of doing impossible things, Knowing few rope tricks, Master trouble shooters, Know-all and **of course, all-in-one!**

We often see in India, several Industry leaders burning the night lamps and staying late in the office, which is essential part of senior management's duties. In fact, many mastered the art of staying late and take it as an excuse to reach office late in the next day. The Time of reaching office is not counted, but the time of leaving the office is an important consideration for the promotion in many organsiations.

Gordon was impatient to conclude "do you mean to say, A leader has to be Acceptable, Charismatic, able to convince, Motivate, and inspire his followers.?" I nodded my head in concurrence.

Management or Natural process?

Gordon seemed amazed at the ability of Indian Leaders and intrigued by Temple management, *Mela* and festival Management. Subsequently we did not meet for few weeks due to work pressure and summer holidays. Finally when we met again after his vacation, Gordon's first question was "how do you people in India manage the Traffic?". I guessed, Gordon must have had a taste of Mumbai traffic.

I shot back "what management?". Gordon was shocked by my counter question. Gordon shook his head in disbelief and asked "do you mean to say, there is no management? or do you say, there is no discipline?" I nodded in my typical Indian way which signifies both "yes" and "No". Gordon persisted his enquiry and asked, "what do you mean? Yes or No or both?". I nodded for the last option. I cleared my throat and answered in a typical voice of a professor, "before we discuss some management principles which are either not appreciated or not applied in many institutions in India, we will discuss two major present problems in India which are unique. They are **"Traffic Management"** and other is **"Time Management"**.

Successful Leaders need in their armour

- Clarity of Thought
- Noble goals and Vision
- Inspiring track record.
- Earning Confidence of followers.
- Blemish less character
- Courage
- Creative problem solving ability
- Above all, Effective communication

Leadership & Management

Instilling an inspiring vision
Getting important things done
Instilling good operational processes

Successful Management styles of India
Author Rajasekhar Polapragada

3

APPLICATION OF MANAGEMENT PRINCIPLES

"To learn and not to do is really not to learn.
To know and not to do is really not to know."

– Stephen R. Covey

Gordon was curious to know why Traffic Management is tough in India. He asked if application is the problem or the principle? Does it mean, Indians do not believe in Order or Discipline? or simply do not want to apply those principles?. I started thinking loud. if application is so simple, why do we need coaches for all the sports? If principles are not important, why do we hire our coaches? Are the principles and application different?

3.1 TRAFFIC MANAGEMENT

The next day, Gordon was more relaxed. It was Sunday and we both were in no hurry for the work. But break-fast meeting became more interesting. Gordon started the discussion "Raj, you mean to say, Traffic Management in India is a failure of principles or application?" I could understand Gordon's obsession with traffic in India. Any new person visiting India from abroad, as soon as he lands, realizes Indian traffic is unique. Not only from antique bullock carts to modern Mercedes ply on the same road, cyclists, autos, cows and even pedestrians for want of foot-paths, compete for their place on Indian roads. Lack of discipline and control is seen on Indian roads which is tackled by many police and govt. organizations and an acceptable solution is still awaited. Some times traffic is used as an excuse for delay in meeting appointments, but general problem is, of stress and uncertainty and of course road safety. Though situation improved with high ways,bursting population nullified the advantage. Traffic problem is absent in villages, where few vehicles ply on roads with migration to cities for employment.

What significance it has got with this book "successful Indian Management styles?". while we discussed some traditional management styles in the last section, we did not consider changes in the time frame. Population in India has reached 1.2 billion and soon India will be most populous country surpassing China. It is not easy with limited financial resources and most important resource called space. How traffic can be managed in India is a million dollar question, which is not in the scope of this book. However, it highlights the application of principles is the key to success.

While United States of America built their first highway as early as in 1930. At that time, India had 300 million population with main trade paths used for centuries augmented by rulers who built roads for their armies. Subsequently, British built some national highways to bring in their goods and export raw materials like cotton, Tobacco, Tea from India, but they are awfully inadequate. India missed the automobile boom which USA saw due to obvious lack of resources. Additionally, migration of people from villages to cities has increased several fold while population of India itself increased by 4 times. Though Several thousands kilometers of high way is added after independence, still it is inadequate to cover the vast country.

I was appalled to see high rate of traffic accidents in India. After observing high standards of safety in oil industry for decades, I realized it is difficult to expect or convince general public to observe safety In India.

Due to lack of resources to maintain their basic needs of countrymen, both state and federal Governments failed in providing public transport. One may call it indiscipline or unsafe act on the part of public, but I call it economic survival. I observed Several family members in the family use one two wheeler. Police are authorized to fine them or take action, but often compassion and corruption prevent them from taking strict action, leaving thousands to go scot free with traffic violations. Many more learn that punishment is meagre or non existing and soon they join the band wagon of undisciplined crowds. That is the back-ground story of traffic problems in India. Till we solve our Traffic problem, reduce accidents and stop loss of lives in traffic accidents, we can not say, we are successful, even if we become super power or developed country.

It is not un-common to see the cases as shown in the picture below.

NOTE: Author suggests to set up teams in Management schools to study the Traffic Management, which will help students as well as authorities to understand the inherent contradictions and behavior problem associated with traffic accidents. *Another interesting thing is 70% city traffic is 2 wheelers and we may need separate lane for them.*

By-pass and Ring Roads

The objective of this book is not to show a solution to traffic problem in India while traffic jams are prevalent even in San Francisco and New York, India has adopted two solutions to get over Traffic problem

1.   By-pass roads

2.   Ring roads.

How these are relevant to principles of management? These traffic solutions are used by successful mangers in many Indian corporate offices.

By-pass technique is used by several bosses and staff to circumvent the normal hierarchy for communication and command. Ring road technique or Round about way is used by staff to give feed back and orders by bosses.

For example, a typical performance review never was or would be a straight forward communication. Bosses try to show better performance rating to staff while actual rating is kept confidential. So does staff members never communicate real problem to their bosses. It is always cooked up stories or a fabricated personal tragedy.

3.1 TIME MANAGEMENT

"Indian punctuality" is an acronym used by many foreigners which indicates many office in India, do not stick to the appointed time. There are some genuine reasons as to why majority of staff cannot manage their time. One is traffic problem and other is extra load of work. Traffic problem is caused by lack of infra-structure and inadequate public transport system. Extra work is due to the fact, less staff and willingness of some staff to accept work far more than their capability. Some employees pick up more work thinking it will make them indispensable and increase their job security. Apart from that, many Indians do not complain late appointments as they consider them as normal. if you look at history, Time was not given high importance till industrial revolution. Indians are no exception.

History of Time

If we delve into history of time, Romans never had Time control. British had time at their disposal and Eat Indian company operated in "colonial India" without any time compulsion and had a luxury of time. Though Sun rises in the East early, East India company officers never started work before 10 AM and closed for lunch till after noon Tea, while Evenings were reserved for relaxation and Tennis. Even after independence, Indian Administrative officers follow British system. Thus there was a general slackness in maintaining Punctuality in some sections of people in India which continued even after Independence.

There are several employees whose Time starts, when Boss arrives and ends when he leaves. This is called "Boss oriented" very much popular in many places. Then there is "Time oriented" when employees arrive to work on time and leave on time. Finally there is a superior view called work oriented view. There are several management books suggesting prioritizing work as Stephen Covey suggested "First thing first", and other techniques do not have much significance as several executives who either have to wait for some body else or match their priorities. Finally Time management boils down to Priorities. But it becomes impossible to manage, when the plate is full resulting in late working for majority of staff.

Management experts tried many techniques to accomplish Time management and Traffic Management in India. However, their efforts were not successful. Many street smart managers used them to justify their own failures and delays. Some even deliberately delayed planning, anticipating time delays by other departments. In fact, it became an epidemic of delays and postponements. Some government projects designated "5 year project plans" which became a colloquial word for delay.

There is a lenient view on ensuring discipline in Time Management which is part of "four principles discussed in next chapter. Lack of compliance to Rule-Book covers Punctuality and Time management, There are several books on Que or lack of discipline (ref. 4, 5). However, there is lack of general public interest in addressing this problem and not many efforts are made by bosses to tackle Time Management,

• INDIAN PUNCTUALITY PRINCIPLES

* If BOSS is late, it is ok. He is Busy.
* If staff are late, they are irresponsible.

If you are on time.,
you have no important job on hand !
If I am late,
I am very Important Person !
This is British India style ! That is why
"Are you a Lord?" is a common phrase,
to question, if any body is late .

Solutions to tackle the problem
* Let us do Net conference !
* No meetings ! –
* Lets do it my way !
- Let us wait for the Boss !
  Others are not as important !
- This is Adopted Indian Style !

© Source : Successful management styles of India
Author: Rajasekhar Polapragada

Both Traffic and Time Management are two examples which explain how a successful system (else where) may not work in India. Then there are some management principles which are not liked or not popular among successful Management. Some managers often consider Communication as avoidable and some staff use silence as a waste of time and effort. Also during thousand years of foreign rule, majority of population did not practice Transparency nor enjoyed freedom of speech. Thus successful managers know, when staff are silent, it does not signify any approval, but may signify disapproval.

4

MANAGEMENT PRINCIPLES NOT POPULAR IN INDIA

> *Knowing is not enough; we must apply.*
> *Willing is not enough; we must do.*
>
> *— Johann Wolfgang von Goethe*

During my daily discussions, once I asked Gordon, "how can you complain to me about India. I am very much an Indian and patriotic too.". I was impressed with Gordon's answer. He said, some people do not mind accepting their weakness and few like you want to correct them. I explained to Gordon a philosophy shared by majority of successful managers, who may not like some practices, but would like to carry on what is required to complete the job.

Continuing our discussion on Traffic management, we wandered into people specific, culture related preferences and dislikes. Some management principles are not appreciated nor applied in India which are given below. We can not say these principles are not important. However, company after company, has ignored or failed to implement these policies. There may be some genuine reasons, but few who have implemented them are successful in private as well as public sector. Those who could not implement the principles either suffered to earn confidence of public, share holders, government and other stake holders.

Management principles not popular in India

some Principles clash with traditional, local and circumstantial and contemporary political situations.

1. Transperancy
2. Succession
3. Empowerment
4. Rule book

source: Successful Management styles of India

Some times, our likes and dislikes may have some thing to do with traditional, local and circumstantial and contemporary political situations. However, there are several excuses for not implementing them such as official reasons and some are real and kept as hidden agenda. *what works in India may work elsewhere. But what works every where may not work in India.* That is one big reason which prompted author to pen this book "successful management styles of India."

Why these 4 Management principles are important?

Truth and Transparency is the only way to earn loyalty of others. Trust of Employees is essential to run an Enterprise. Trust of share holders is the key to raise capital. Government has to earn Trust of public. A private body which is an imaginary personality generates the loyalty of employees and thus becomes an Enterprise or a corporation. It is trust a corporation earns from the Government, which accords the special privileges to apply company act to treat a corporation like a citizen. Corporations in turn, help public by distributing their profits and offering service. In democracy, a public trust is synonymous with Trust of government, which is dependent on Transparency.

Succession plan ensures continuity of any corporation. In fact, even for an individual, succession means family. As man is not immortal, so do corporations. Hence succession plan is essential for the long term viability of any organization.

Empowerment helps ease of operation as well as higher output is possible only by Empowerment. It is pre requisite or logical step to Succession. Many succession plans fail due to failure of implementing work delegation and Empowerment. Empowerment is essential for succession plan like flowering and fruits are essential for survival of a tree.

Finally **Compliance or following the Rule-Book** is essential to maintain mutual benefit of society and Enterprise which in turn helps society to live in peace. Following Rule-Book is essential for business to prosper and enterprises to co-exist and work for the benefit of society. This is possible by avoiding covet and corrupt operations.

However,

1. Transparency is often confused with Confidentiality and some times it is used to hide real intentions of top bosses.

2. Succession is often delayed due to lack of team building and reluctance of top management to loose the control.

3. Empowerment is often not favored due to lack of confidence in staff due to incompetency of staff or inadequate Training. Thus supervisor's lack of confidence in staff and some times, lack of self confidence is also a reason for not empowering staff.

4. Rule book is not followed due to general indiscipline or un-limited freedom at all levels. There is another big reason for non compliance, which is un-ethical or selfish. What ever may the reason, if Rule -book is not followed, all have to suffer.

Inter-relation of all 4 principles

It creates more problems and problems cascade, If one of the 4 principles is not followed, other Principles are broken one by one and eventually a corporation, society or even government collapses. Like a puzzle, we have to start at one point. That should start at the top of the organization as buck stops at the top.

As we all saw one Prime Minister changed as Modi took over and whole nation has changed its perception. So far, many thought there is no solution to corruption. But with two ex chief ministers (one from Haryana and other from Bihar) were sent to jail, Indian voters started thinking it is possible to prosecute even a person occupying highest position. More important with the right change at top, it is possible for every body to follow the rule book.

If Transparency is followed, staff and public can question any wrong doings, or omissions or commissions can be exposed. Succession plan can be announced for the eligible candidates. Unless Empowerment is done, development of staff is not complete and final Succession is not possible.. if rule book is followed, all three principles can be followed including Transparency. As per latest report of SEBI (Stock Exchange Bureau of India), about top 200 companies in India have yet to split the roles of MD and Chairman. This speaks volumes of succession and Empowerment in Indian Enterprises. What is the implication of this? Chairman plays the role of the owner representing share holders. MD or Managing Director makes it viable through vision, plan and process. When these two positions are single, Transparency is not possible and it is difficult to know if the enterprise is in real trouble or it is used to get personal gain of owners. No wonder many Indian business men evade loans when in trouble, park money in Tax havens when company performs well. Thus general share holders are at loss both ways. There is no check on personal gains nor sister companies which thrive like parasites on the main companies. What happened during British rule was both rulers and traders were same with East India company at helm of affairs. It can be seen in rise of UK from 3% to 30% of world GDP during their rule of India, while Indian GDP fell from 23% to 2% in 2000 years. It takes centuries for India to correct this. The purpose of this book is to highlight the wide spread practices and remedies for the same. The four management principles which are not favored by Indian business Leaders are Transparency, Succession plan, Empowerment and avoiding (not following) Rule-book.

4.1 TRANSPARENCY

According to a report by Transparency International (TI), a Berlin-based anti-corruption watchdog, Indian firms are most transparent among emerging market peers from among emerging market firms. Nine Indian firms Airtel, Mahindra, Wipro, and six Tata firms feature in Transparency International's list of top 10 most transparent companies from emerging markets. That statistics, which may seem ironic in a country where large-scale corporate scams and frauds are not uncommon. It is only to be expected, say analysts, because several of India's blue-chip companies have adopted transparent and globally accepted and recognized Foreign Investments soared high in those stocks. Also few companies like TATAs, Infosys were listed in New York stock exchanges and are governed by their rules and follow well established accounting standards and processes. These companies will be covered in the volume 2 of the Tri series "Successful management Practices of India". While in principle, all agree for Transparency, in practice several street - smart companies think, in the short term, they can manage without Transparency. Let us probe the history which also contributed to lack of Transparency among few small and medium companies.

History

While industrialization is not older than 2 centuries, Indian Business culture was more influenced by British. British rulers used diplomacy to control vast Indian subcontinent. Hence confidentiality instead of Transparency, was their main tool to rule India with multi faiths and variety of races and religions. It worked well with their policy of "Divide and Rule". Many Indian managers as it suited them, continued the policy of non-transparency. This lack of Transparency is not limited only to top management; even lower level staff would hide information from the management.

I have a first hand information from a senior HR executive on this subject. Two decades back, I was invited by a large corporation in India to join them in their maiden refinery project. As soon as I got down from their private jet, this HR executive Mr. Bhatt (name is changed) came to receive me. I asked Mr. Bhatt, "while so many qualified engineers are existing in India, why did they prefer experts from abroad?" Mr. Bhatt simply replied "it is our observation that many Indian executives push the problems under the carpet. Often we come to know of the disaster only after the problem becomes too big to resolve". It is a classic example for lack of Transparency.

Till Bosses stop the attitude of "shooting the messenger", Transparency is difficult to achieve. But who will bell the cat? TOP executives of the management, not executives.

why some Indian mangers do not favor transparency?

1.   To retain their power in the board room.

2.   The fear of competition from rivals and sense of insecurity among senior employees.

3.   *Lack of responsibility among work force and lack of accountability* who misuse information.

Unless there is a general demand from staff or public or share holders, it is difficult for top management themselves implementing Transparency. However, In the long term viability, sustainability and globalization, Transparency is a must though it is not favored by successful managers in India. While Succession and Empowerment affect company performance, Transparency and Not following Rule-Book affects Society. It was discovered between 2014-2016, when government had to de-recognize more than 200,00 directors and as many corporations were de-registered for not filing Income Tax or not filing renewal of corporate registration with government of India. That shows the gravity of situation. However, it also shows several CEOs did not favor or support or followed Transparency.

There is no need to emphasize the need for implementing which help other 3 principles. In fact, the inter dependency is clearly observed in the blame game in not implementing Transparency than in other 3 management principles.

Ring Road strategy (Mis-Information)

Many times, top management does not give straight answers or gives a misleading explanations while side lining staff from main duties and responsibilities. "It is not uncommon to transfer staff to Safety or Training departments, as a punishment. This indicates two things. Neither training nor that person is important in the eyes of management. That is confirmed by the budget as well as low importance given for review of Safety and training departments. Other neglected departments in India is Research and Development. While these 3 or 4 areas are neglected, it is an indication how transparency is flouted by the top bosses. Feed-back information is given to staff in a round-about fashion. Often these actions lead to resignation of staff.

Now let us see, how staff use this Ring-Road strategy to mis-lead management. Whenever feed back or data is required by management, staff give flimsy reasons or lame excuses for not giving authentic data. Remember! HR executive of a top Indian company explained me, that many senior executives have tendency to suppress the disaster news and shove the problems under carpet which have a potential to derail the project or destabilize the organization. This is done to just safe-guard their jobs and incidentally completes the cycle of "mis–information" (in the name of confidentiality) passed on to them from top.

The focus of this book is on corporations giving mis-information or hiding the data or not being Transparent. We are all aware of main reason for bankruptcy of Enron and others who suppressed their data and Mis-information which wiped them. Non-Transparency is dangerous to the health of the company. In India,, in a recent review RBI found NPA (Non Performing Assets) of nationalized Banks far exceeded the allowed norms. Some are communication gaps, some are deliberate suppression of facts. This is observed in almost all departments of Federal government.

Another example is statistics such as unemployment figures which are never reliable. As India is an agricultural economy till recently, many jobs are seasonal. This puts a big question mark on all press releases by company as well as government statistics. Even RTI act (Right To Information) which is not effective due to this wide spread malice. **Thus successful Indian Managers need to learn how to manage or filter mis-information and this is one technique developed by many successful leaders in India.** What they do? They meet staff from all layers of organization. It is done more effectively by family business houses.

Lack of Team spirit or Unity: This is some thing which makes India unique or probably comparable to few countries like United States of America, where multi cultures, multi races and multi religions exist at one place. It resulted in several views on how to resolve an issue. Thus different opinions cause disunity. It might happen in other parts of world also. **But what makes India unique is we welcome the different views and will not try to silence the dissent. That is one reason, India is the only country, where revolution is always silent and it takes some times centuries to develop a consensus.** While cultural diversity is welcome, transparency is the first victim in this atmosphere. In business world, there is competition driven confidentiality, it is common to maintain secrecy even among small groups. This is the reason why benevolent dictatorship is appreciated as it does not involve ruthless suppression of dissent.

As relations are important in India, Transparency is thought by many as hindrance to maintain good relations. In summary, due to lack of trust, unity and to maintain good relations, Transparency is sacrificed.

Famous Indian Crab Story: There is a famous crab story, to illustrate the disunity in India. The famous British policy of "divide and Rule" is made easy in India, while "division" is already existing, "rule" is only required. British could rule India with a population as large as 10 times British island. Let me share the story, of course, it may be fictitious or a joke. There was a competition among all nations about, which country has largest size of crabs. Every country sent their box full of crabs, with a lid and small holes so that crabs can breath.

At the same time, the holes are not big enough so that crabs can not escape. While Africa won the competition, every one was surprised to see Indian contingency sent the box full of crabs without a lid. Why? Answer is simple. Whenever a crab goes up, remaining crabs pull that crab and it repeats whichever crab tries to escape. So why to waste money on the lid? It is a classic "Jugad" (Indian word for innovation). Though the story is a joke, it aptly describes the 28 states and 8 Union Territories in India with as many languages and all the religions of the world. Each one has its own priorities and think other group is progressing better. There is a common feeling each one is struggling to be successful. It some times creates competition, some times frustration and mostly comparison. So sharing of information is considered special only for close groups.

Some companies especially family run businesses do not share the information except with insiders. The result is cautious sharing of information, which is definitely not Transparency. Even top executive some times do not know the direction in which the company moves. Some times, even staff also hide the information for which no serious action is taken. In short, hiding information is not viewed as a serious problem.

4.2 SUCESSION PLAN

Many Indian leaders do not nominate or plan a successor. It is not uncommon to see large corporations struggle to select a successor or some times a wrong successor and take corrective action later.

One of the largest Indian conglomerate Tata Sons with over USD 100 dollars turn over owns Tata group of companies, Tata Consultancy services, Tata steel, and owners of international brands like Jagaur, Titley Tea, Land rover, Tata Moors etc. experienced successor problem. Few years back,, they selected Cyrus Mistry as successor to *Ratan Tata*. Later as they found conflicting interests and it took great efforts to remove Cyrus from the board. A similar experience was with IT giant Infosys in naming successor to *Narayana* murthy. If this is the case with large corporations, imagine the plight of other Indian companies.

Older generation refuses to hang their boots

One of the problems is older generation refusing to relinquishing their power. Power hungry bosses are present every where including India. But if you look at political leaders in Inida, many successors appeared only after the demise of the leader. It is not uncommon to see a Prime Minister or President in India in his late 80's, *Morarjee Desai* became PM of India in 1977, at the age of 85. Except Rajiv Gandhi, none of the PMs were less than 60. Ratan Tata fixed 75 as maximum age for directors of Tata companies. Many directors of Indian corporate dons are above 70 vs much younger CEOs in USA. In few family owned companies, succession wars between brothers and children and parents are recorded. All this points out to lack of clear cut succession policy which is an age old problem of India.

Ancient India

why is Succession is not a well documented in the rule book nor followed in Indian corporate world? Let us go deeper in to the past Indian culture, As per the oldest document *Ramayan*, when king *Dasarath* was about to announce his eldest Son *SriRam* as his successor, his youngest wife *Kaikeya* suggested her son Bharat as the future King. There was no war, but *SriRam* was sent out in exile so that succession will be smooth. Though *Dasarath* did not like it, succession as per his choice was not followed. Next Epic MahaBharat had a more tricky story on succession. Blind King Dhrutarashtra was an appointed royal dignitary and his son *Suyodhan* was not eligible to succeed to throne. Genuine eligible person to the throne was Udhistur who challenged it and it was resolved only after a greatest war which involved almost all kings of India. Here again succession problem. And of course, several countries will have these succession wars, but what makes India unique is it is not war alone, but two epics are written and discussed and debated by all.

Result is that it makes it tough for the corporations and public to accept the new successor unless it is done confidentially or by consensus or out of necessity due to death or any eventuality. As it takes a very long time to arrive at consensus, many resorted to path of Confidentiality and secrecy.

Modern India

Interestingly, several Prime Ministers in India took over from their predecessors with almost no experience in the job. When Indira Gandhi was assassinated by her own body guards, her son Rajiv Gandhi took over as Prime Minister with no experience even as a minister in the Cabinet. Even Indira Gandhi took over as PM when her predecessor Lal Bahadur Sastry died in Russia in a suspecting circumstances. The same scenario is reflected in Indian corporate world also.

India's, biggest business conglomerate TATAs had a legend Ratan Tata as their chairman. Ratan Tata has succeeded in globalizing Tatas. But his elevation which was in 1980's was not an easy process. Ratan Tata was adopted by Jamshedji Tata, father of Indian Industrialization. Yet, Ratan Tata had to go through a tough 25 years journey cum training. Later, Ratan Tata had to confront giants like Russi Modi and Mulagoankar. who were heading Tata Steel and TELCO, respectively.

By-passing

Often we find big bosses contacting, directing lower rank staff and delegate the work. Other times, staff have multiple loyalties and priority of work is affected by this strategic by-pass which is covered in 4th principle called "non compliance or not following rule book".

One big problem which many leaders complain regarding "by-passing' problem, is lack of competency among staff. Some Staff think, it is easier to climb corporate ladder by-passing the boss and contacting big boss. As a result "Trust" is missing among many and often is the main reason for not implementing "Succession chart. Also secrecy and lack of trust are inter related and hinder implementing succession plan. In short, hurdles for Empowerment are same as hurdles for Succession.

Multi –hierarchy and multi-tasking is a big problem to train successors in several areas of expertise. On a positive side, by-passing is done by bosses, in search of a competent successor, as immediate successor is not capable or lack drive and enthusiasm to progress. Even if you find a successor, in India, it is difficult to name the best person as successor as Loyalty is an accepted criterion. Loyalty is defined differently by different people, some define it as integrity, some consider it for the company, few consider it for individuals.

B. Team building

Another reason cited by managers for not announcing successor is lack of cohesion among team players which is reflected in several fronts. For example, National teams like cricket and hockey and even Olympic teams have some times official and some time unofficial representation of regions is a big concern. If a successor is announced, mostly acceptability is a problem and divisions among teams as well as lobbying starts mostly on the basis of regional, language. It is an un necessary distraction for the company while successor may not evolve or raise to the occasion based on performance or other considerations. So many CEOs keep succession details confidential which again points to lack of transparency,which in their opinion keeps team spirit in tact. Though long term credibility build up measures have to be taken up, many avoid them as they are time consuming like Training and coaching which takes time is now being taken up as priority.

C. Hurdles for implementing Succession plan

- Lack of proper recruiting procedures and empowerment practice to test the probable candidates.

- Many Leaders feel lack of accountability to share holders prompts power hungry leaders who, stick to their seat, want to give reins of the corporations to their nominees/children.

- General excuse given by Leaders is lack of strong Team spirit and lack of acceptable candidates.

4.3 EMPOWERMENT

Several management books discussed at length the difference between delegation and Empowerment. While delegation is handing-over of job or work, empowerment provides the power to acquire resources as well as helps to develop responsibility and accountability. Thus Empowerment works as stepping stone for Succession plan.

Many successful Managers in India are reluctant to empower their staff, as they are NOT confident that their subordinates are capable of handling independently. That shows on one side, less efforts by Leaders to develop their staff and inadequate training opportunities. On the other side, less efforts by staff to learn and less enthusiasm to improve their skills. Biggest complaint by staff is that they do not get opportunities to test their abilities. Unless staff are entrusted jobs and carry out independently, they can not have real time experience of dealing with situations. As a result, Empowerment is not very popular in many companies. However, IT companies and those enterprises who are in service industry are forced to empower their staff to fulfil their commitment to customers.

Succession and Empowerment inter relation

In fact, succession and Empowerment are related, if not 100% dependent on each other. Without a clear cut succession policy, Empowerment has no legitimacy nor logical conclusion. Without Empowerment, it is difficult to choose a right candidate internally, who understands company policies and values and from internal sources. In highly visible companies, like Apple and Microsoft, succession plans are watched with interest. Every succession plan may not be successful as it was in case of Tim Hook and Nadella. Now imagine, without a succession policy and Transparency, what will be success rate in the Indian corporate world? Probably Empowerment is the best starting point for Succession. However, if management are either not clear or not transparent, it is much more difficult. Let us see some genuine reasons or hurdles to Empowerment in Indian context.

4.3.1 Delegation and Reverse-delegation (Up-delegation)

It is a unique feature in India, staff resort to reverse delegation or up-delegation. What is "up-delegation? it is the reverse of delegation." Instead of work flowing from top to bottom, it flows upward. That means staff assign back, their work to bosses. One wonders why bosses accepted this up-delegation?.

Some bosses gladly take up the work left by their staff. They would like to do all the jobs which will get them job security. Some bosses are forced to do it as they lack confidence in their staff. Other interesting aspect is Staff give part of their work load to their bosses either because they are not capable or they know their job is secure, in the absence of "Hire &Fire" policy. Normally, in many companies, no clear description of roles and responsibilities is written or followed. Even if they are part of Rule-book, many staff leave the work as it is NOT considered violation of duty. Many bosses, accept extra work as part of their work. Hard work and over-time is considered necessary to go up in the organizational ladder in Indian corporate world..

Many believe, leaders are appreciated for their hard work, if not accepted for their ability and competence. We can categorize leaders as Lions or Ants based on their acceptability levels. Many Indians like their Leaders to be hardworking. If need arises, a Leader has to be a like a Lion and spearhead the opposition by leading from the front. Some times, a leader acts like ant, doing all the sundry work to compensate for the inabilities of staff.

A Leader has to be like an ANT in many respects .
➢ Look at minute things for Quality
➢ Hardworking for Results
➢ Be self- disciplined to ensure discipline
➢ Community work for Bonding
➢ and above all Honest for developing Trust .

© ABCD of Leadership –
A for ANT

At this point, Gordon interrupted " do you mean to say a CEO has to work like an Ant? But I prefer to work like a Lion". I chose to answer Gordon by narrating my experience than a straight YES or NO. It was during my stay in a public sector Oil company which was originally a Multi national company and later was nationalized. My boss who was a hard working person, who came-up from ranks. He used to be the first person to reach the office and stay late at office, to finish all his work. He used to thoroughly review his subordinate's work and some times do their work as well.

"Reverse-delegation" of work is unavoidable in the case of shortage of staff and resources. Some successful managers knew how to deal with it and developed norms and "Roles and Responsibilities". But inadequate staff and low efficiency related to low salaries are real problems faced by many companies in India.

4.3.2 Responsibility and Accountability

If I have to name two things which are conspicuously absent in post independent India, it is lack of Responsibility and Accountability. One may argue it is an off-shoot of 1000 years of foreign rule or lack of education. It is not True as many great Leaders are born during freedom fight and Gandhi, Nehru to name a few. In my opinion, the main reason is mostly to avoid blame, in case they fail. That puts more burden on leaders to accept slack performance of subordinates and take extra burden of responsibility. In a country where thousands sacrificed their lives for achieving freedom, it is an irony, we ended up with many persons, even in high positions who shun accountability. It can be attributed to unlimited freedom after independence resulting in not following Rule-book. This attitude of indiscipline, if not encouraged, at least NOT deterred by Benevolent Leadership. For example, out of compassion, many employers do not favor "hire and fire" which gives a feeling of job security to employees. Few take it as a blessing, but many misuse this and take advantage of this compassion. It is this majority who bring down the standard of work ethics. To avoid the bad reputation, it is a common practice from top to bottom to play the "blame game". One remedy, Management does compensates for the in-efficiency is assigning more employees for the task and correspondingly at lower salaries. Thus less qualified and less experienced employees fill the employee chart. **Thus a crowd is created, NOT a team.** This is a perfect mix for lack of accountability. If any employee is responsible and works hard and he is not compensated, he will look for lucrative offers. There are several companies who always look for hard working employees and more than the qualification, those who show responsibility bag the job offer. Unfortunately, another menace is recommendations and internal struggle which worsens the quality of working teams. *A successful management has to keep a tab on the coterie and internal groups which are formed by language, caste and other narrow definitions, basically to cover each other from blame game.*

One of the reasons given by Business Leaders for not favoring Delegation and Empowerment is lack of responsibility assumed by staff. It hampers delegation of work, which in-turn does not give scope of Empowerment. If one hesitates to delegate, that will become hindrance to Empowerment. It is a catch 22 situation. As a result many business leaders are over burdened and take more work and responsibility than one can handle. This leaves less time for them to do planning, strategy and even hamper their creativity. *But bosses are equally to be blamed for not able to fix accountability on erring staff.*

ABCD of Delegation

I - Interest - Ichcha sakti
A – Ability – Jnana sakti
S - skill – Kriya Sakti
IAS is the success formula
of Delegation !
The enemy of Delegation is
Blame.

Delegate !   Blame !

Delegation does not take away our Responsibility to complete the job.
Blamers can never delegate. So spot those who play Blame game, and remover them from job.
This is the single obstacle in in improving Indian management style.
Right from political leaders to Corporate czars, all blame others.
From chairman to chaprasi many Indians love to play the blame game.
IAS officers blame politicians though they are given full responsibility and authority.

© ABCD of Leadership   www. Economic Engineering Excellence.org

Developing staff is one problem and taking responsibility is other problem. Together they are bane of Empowerment. One solution can be following basic principles of developing staff and those who can not or do not want to take responsibility can be removed from the list of succession chart.

Compassion: if compassion is not discussed, we will miss a key factor in Indian management tradition. it is not uncommon to find employees pleading on the grounds of large family or lack of money during serious discussion of performance appraisal. We have to remember the two games played daily by employees.

One is "Blame game". Other is "personal sad stories". Every day, when my staff miss a target or late to the office, I used to ask for an explanation. In variably, they turn out to be a personal excuse than a professional explanation. This is true from watchman to chairman. What is surprising is the "if you do not listen the story, you are nick-named stone hearted.

Gordon was curious how I handled these situations. I had to share my secret. That is not to ask for explanation than to waste my time listing to the "tell tales of troubles".

4.3.3 Training and Development

One of the reasons Business leaders in India point out is Insufficient funds. Genrally, in many corporations, inadequate interest is shown in Training and safety related departments, at all management levels. Development of staff is inadequate in many corporations and this can be deducted by two observations.

1. Low budget for Training

2. Succession manuals and road map for at least senior management staff are not made available to the employees.

How to Develop staff ?

Economic Engineering Excellence

Can they do it ?
Augment team by hiring qualified members. Best practice is doing it !

Are they trained to do?
Give continuous training !

Do they want to do it ?
Inspire , not just Motivate !

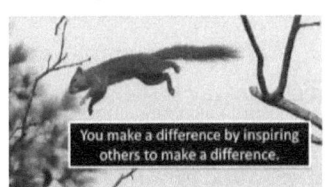

You make a difference by inspiring others to make a difference.

There is a general attitude among many Indians, that physical work is a low level of work and to be avoided. That applies to all levels of employees and any development jobs are seen in that light. Both training and development is not preferred by many employees compared to high visibility jobs.

4.3.4 Recruitment and Retaining

Some other reasons, though not common, are less qualification, less suitability and less ability or less experience are some problems faced in private sector. In Public sector, interference of Government and bureaucracy has derailed the succession plans.

As many employees complain lower salaries as a reason for less motivation, some managers believe, lack of inspiring leaders also deprive employees of challenging assignments.

Absence of policy of Hire & Fire

Due to absence of "Hire & Fire" policy, the quality of employees can not be controlled. Hence management resorts to shifting employees to areas of less priority which is done by frequent transfers. Though it is part of management responsibility of staffing, many managers feels their hands are tight due to lack of accountability and responsibility at all levels compounded by absence of "Hiring and firing" policy.

Interestingly, in India neither government nor employees and not even senior management like firing of employees. Instead of firing, some managers resort to transfers. IAS officers evolved a system to motivate or threaten employees by using transfers as a management tool. There is popular phrase called "Transfer to Timbuctoo", a remote town located in Africa. It seems, some British officer was transferred to Africa as a punishment. Andamans is another place to transfer the staff who do not perform. But sacking of staff is a big NO. It is not that employees will not get terminated, but many times, the round about way is shown to the employees than to sack them. Exceptions are there, If a disciplinary action or an action which is necessitated by a rule, anti social or moral grounds backed by a large section of public. We will see an example of this in next chapter.

Some of the ring-road techniques which I mentioned earlier are applied. In stead of sacking, employees are side-lined which is done in many companies world wide. Other one is transfers to safety or environment or some critical, yet neglected departments by the management. In latter case, in mistake will entitle them for a severe action. In fact safety incidents are taken care by the federal or industries department and few realize that they are not in good books of management unless they have no other option....... This reluctance to sack employees and lack of bankruptcy policies (till few year back) for Enterprises,helped to accumulate lot of slack performance in India. Latter problem is solved after 2014, when Bankruptcy act was changed to accommodate enterprises to close down their shop.

Different policies in different sectors

Public sector units have a long process of written test and interview. Many times it is tough to get job in public sector units than private sector. However in many public sector and government departments, recommendation play a part. Some time appraisals are not transparent and fair. If appraisals are not fair, we create two problems. Meritorious employees start leaving organization or start under-performing. In a Process which equate donkeys and horses are treated same way, horses go away. That is what happened with many PSUs.

Some successful Mangers have introduced Mentoring to develop the staff.

Another factor noticed by successful Leaders is that it takes considerable time to Train a suitable person for succession. Often loyalty and ability do not match empowerment. Thus 4 steps and 4 hurdles are highlighted by successful Mangers of India.

Key steps to Succession:

1. Share the vision

2. Make an open announcement and look at all levels,not just one level low.)

3. start early

4. offer Training and feed back.

Hurdles to Succession:

1. Leaders hanging on to power.

2. Lack of Empowerment culture

3. Lack of eligible candidates.

4. lack of Training

4.4 COMPLIANCE TO THE RULE-BOOK

Many Successful Indian corporate Leaders do not follow rule book....... Their justification for not following Rule -Books can be summed up as given below.

-   Lack of consistent Govt. policies till Economic reforms initiated in 1991 and there after lack of long term policies defined by India centric Economic considerations.

-   High level of corruption and uncertainty which makes impossible to run the corporations on long term plans.

-   Big role of personal influence and recommendation in govt, as well as society which require special skills and charisma to win over divergent views.

- Many unqualified and untrained professionals occupying high positions who do not respect a policy or predictable path.

Thus leadership has to be different and yet acceptable and Right which makes Indian Management style a real risky profession like mountaineering and each one has to learn his own skills to reach the top.

Successful Leaders take situational stand
Good Leaders take People stand.
Great Leaders take principle stand !

Stand by your team till they are right
Support people as long as they respect all !

Continue to be Leader if you have to
compromise with People's behaviour !

Stop being a Leader if you have to
compromise with principles !

©Polapragada Self Reliance

© ABCD of Leadership

"Sometimes you need to look at Life from a different perspective."

A leader has to think differently from
But has to be right at the same time.
©helpyoursociety

Threat of Nationalization of private industry

It is not just Businessmen of India, but even federal government does not follow the Rule-Book. This resulted in inconsistent policies such as government take over of private industries. This is seen as a big threat for industrialists to invest their money. It started with suspension of privy purses to erstwhile Maharajas. Nehru, the first prime Minister of India had a vision of both govt. and private industry. His daughter Indira Gandhi, had a socialistic view who nationalized Banking industry and Oil Industry. Apart from fluctuating world economic scene and general business risk etc.. one of the main problems Indian businessmen faced was threat of Nationalization. This situation continued till Economic reforms took place in 1991.

4.4.1 Multi-Loyalty

Trust was not developed between Business Men and Government. This is the case between owners and employees and bosses and staff which is accepted

instead of tackled. Gordon asked me if Trust or lack of it is the reason for not giving him free hand. I told Gordon, it is because several top executives who are close to the owners have access to the chairman and they have multi loyalty. Gordon wanted to know what is this Multi loyalty?. I explained that India is only country, where revolution did not take place. Old thoughts and new thoughts co-exist. If parasites live on the tree, they not only weaken the tree, but consume a portion of what we feed the plant. So also, some employees, have multi-loyalty, but they can not be sacked due to missing "hire and - Fire policy. Even if Interests of Share holders are not represented by CEOs, many CEOs are NOT sacked in India. In many public listed companies shares quote at low values as public doubt the loyalty of promoters.. In Public sector, government (in real terms some vested ruling party members call the shots) interference with working. This interference of government in PSUs can be part due to no accountability or not following Rule-book. Interestingly bureaucrats with no back-ground of business give the directions in Public sector corporations. one example is Air India, a blue chip company nationalized by Government of India (taken over from Tatas) is presently at the stage of insolvency as no body wants to even buy it, when federal government wants to sell it. Several private companies syphon money from the companies and divert to some shell companies with connivance of politicians. With recent change in policy of Bankruptcy laws and mergers and acquisitions are possible. But in general multi loyalty among Business leaders, staff make it tough to follow "Rule-Book".......
In some cases, environment and safety rules are flouted but no accountability is not fixed in many cases or actions not taken. in 1984, Union Carbide case is a glaring example, where 3000 people died and 12000 were crippled while courts could not fix the responsibility though no body followed "Rule-Book".

When loyalty of CEO towards share holders is in doubt, share value of the company goes down. One of the reasons for low Index at Bombay Stock market, till recently is lack of public confidence in both public and private companies. Once few companies registered with New York Stock Exchange, things started moving in the right direction. Thus Transparency and efficiency are driving forces for market capitalization.

4.4.2 Un-limited freedom

Gordon wondered, in a country, where education levels were not high, sense of freedom is unusually high. I shared with him, one story my father used to tell me....... in 1947, when India obtained independence, an old woman was found walking in the middle of the road. When police questioned her, she replied," today we got independence". The magistrate while announcing fine said" if you have freedom to walk in the middle of road, a truck driver also got unlimited freedom to run over you ". This sums up the situation in corporate circles till few years back. As many did not file income tax returns, nor registered their companies and as a result 200,00 directors lost their job and more than 200,000 companies lost their license between 2014-2017. This give a fair picture of the gravity of problem what I call as "Un Limited Freedom".

I turned to Gordon and asked him, "if un-limited freedom is not enough, there are many employees who are more loyal to kingdom, than the king. It may give an answer why the person who recruited you is creating hurdles for you". Gordon nodded his head, as he learnt Indian way of nodding head, to say "Yes" while signaling to say "No".

Before concluding this chapter I would say, Successful managers in India knew how to deal with all these problems or try to circumvent some and leave rest of them to their bosses to manage.

4.4.3 Hidden agenda

Many times, all powerful CEOs would think they have limitless powers or they think they have unlimited Freedom. Some times they have hidden agenda which may not necessarily always be ethical. Performance issues are dogging the corner suites across companies as more CEOs got fired than ever before for ethical lapses in 2018, even as their tenures have gotten shorter since the turn of the millennium, according to the latest report on CEO performance. **Ethically right?** While the share of CEOs booted out from office last year wasn't anywhere near the all time high in this century — 5.1% in 2008 — it's still the highest in the 10 year period between 2009 and 2018. More importantly, of the total number of CEO who were sacked, 2018 saw the highest number of these corner office occupants being shown the door for ethical, rather than financial reasons. That the moral compass of a company's commander-in-chief has been weakening has been evident over the years — between 2007 and 2016, there was a 36% rise in CEOs fired for ethical lapses, from 3.9% in the period between 2007-2011 to 5.3% between 2012-2016. Examples of ethical misconduct include fraud, bribery, insider trading, environmental disasters, inflated resumes and other indiscretions.

The above phenomenon is all over the world, India is not an exception. which is not focus of this book. I explained to Gordon, while India is facing all the problems which world is facing, there are some unique issues in India which we suffer additionally. Hidden agenda is not limited to India but it is a global phenomenon.

Not following Rule book

Many Leaders do not follow rule book due to .

1. lack of consistent Govt. policies

2. High level of corruption and uncertainty

3. Big role of personal influence and recommendation which require special skills and charisma to win over divergent views .

4.Many unqualified and untrained professional occupying high positions who do not respect a policy or predictable path.

Thus leadership Ladder has become like mountaineering and each one has to learn his own skills to reach top.

4 A's Acceptability, Ability, Adoptability, and Adjustability

Gordon was amazed and asked a familiar question. "Raj, why do you think your situation is different from other places?' I said," every one thinks they are unique. But acceptability and adoptability varies with situations. Ability and Adoptability are in leader's domain. Gordon wondered aloud" who has adjust, public, or government or corporations? Let us see how Indian corporations dealt with these four management principles and survived.

Some score high in Transparency, some focus on Succession policy, few on Empowerment and mostly fumble on Rule book. Every corporation is unique in handling the issues. However, till the Indian economic reforms were introduced in 1991, companies had to live with License and Permit Raj when they had to focus on Transparency and Rule Book. Subsequently they focused more on Empowerment and Succession. while there are several issues with corporations, we limit this book to only these 4 principles,with some related issues such as Responsibility and Accountability

Ultimately, ability is next to acceptability as the additional qualification to be leader. Gordon asked " what more takes to be a Leader to be Acceptable in India? '. I was ready with my answer "4A's "Acceptability", Ability, Adjustability and Adoptability."

PART-II

INDIAN MANAGEMENT STYLE PRIOR TO ECONOMIC REFORMS IN 1991

India is the cradle of Human race, the birthplace of Human speech, the mother of History, the grandmother of legend and the great grand mother of tradition. Our most valuable and most constructive materials in the history of man are treasured up in India only

– Mark Twain

5

TRANFORMING AN AMERICAN COMPANY TO INDIAN STYLE.......

> *"Every reform movement has a lunatic fringe."*
>
> *– Theodore Roosevelt*

Summer is usually, very hot in western India, where our project site was located. But mornings are pleasant. During one summer Sunday morning, while we were having our breakfast, Gordon remembered the great Indian leaders. He wondered, how present Indian leaders compared to the legends of past. I told Gordon, given the complexity of India, it is difficult for any leaders to be acceptable pan India. India itself is not a country, but a continent. I thought, it was difficult to explain Gordon the complexity of India, with 28 states, 200 languages and 20 odd scripts where almost all the world religions are active and respected. Additionally India, being world's largest democracy with a free press, every person having a different view on every issue and also many are not just vocal but some times violent in expression (called *dharnas* and *bandhs* means force closing schools and shops) to express their view point. Leave-alone bringing them on to one line of thinking, even understanding India is equal to understanding the world. To make it simple, I thought it is better to share my own experience prior to 1991 and let Gordon deduct his own conclusion. it also might give a glimpse of Indian scenario prior to Economic reforms. This was my story starting after my graduation in Chemical Engineering. I joined an American Oil company which was nationalized later. The decade I stayed in that company, till I left it, also covers the period (1980-1991) when several policy changes were taken by Indian government. I told Gordon "what you see to-day is a lot different than what I saw when I left India,

2 decades back." I told him, how an American Oil company I worked, was slowly changed and brought to Indian style of working. Gordon was curious to know how an American oil company was Indianized.

Nationalization of Indian Oil Industry: Between 1950-60, during the regime of Prime Minister Nehru, foreign oil companies Burma Shell, Caltex and Esso, were invited to establish their operations in India. Subsequently between 1970-80, Nehru's daughter Indira Gandhi, who leaned to socialist pattern to help the poor, nationalized Banking sector and foreign oil companies in a span of short time. I worked in one of these companies, whose name is kept confidential for the sake of liberty of expression. The incidents are real and give a glimpse of change in management style. It is interesting to see some following old management techniques while others adopt to time tested Indian values of compassion and patience; few following old discipline, others trying to implement public sector policies inspired by socialistic pattern of society. One refinery was located in a city in Eastern India. Other was in western India. In one location, canteen for workers and management staff used to be same.; While in Bombay we had different canteen for staff and officers. Both places had different management styles. While at one place, Indianization was quick, at other location, it was slow. At one location, staff were dedicated and had loyalty to the workplace while in another location, employees were result oriented and disciplined. In one location, workers used to go for frequent strikes and officers worked with team spirit. In other location, work was smooth while many employees resigned for better prospects. While management struggled to implement discipline at one place, at other place, retention of qualified engineers was the problem.

My idea was not to cover all the aspects of management, but the areas of Human resources such as recruiting, retaining talent, Leadership including Transparency, following Rule book, empowerment and Succession.

Dream job

Gordon was curious to know my first hand account. I was also enthusiastic to re-live my graduation days and lessons I learnt. Like all youngsters, I had a dream to get a decent job. Decent job was defined as a posting with four figure salary. There were not many companies who gave a four figure salary to a fresh engineering graduate those days. We had a petroleum refinery and a fertilizer company in the city where I studied my engineering. I knew if I stood among the first few in my batch, I could get summer training in an American refining company. Best part of the job in American oil company was the life style and facilities, a nice club, beach side camping, restaurants with Ice cream and coke at subsidized rates, nice lunch at canteen! who does not want to go to that refinery for training, which had restaurant, like a 5 star hotel?

At Sea side club, just across the university campus, a different world, with club, tennis, swimming pools, Airconditioned bungalows, life is a luxury jaunt, if we join the American oil company. We used to steal our week ends with some of our friends whose dads used to work there to spend a day at swimming and high tea in the club.

Sea side Club.......

Merit or Recommendation for recruitment?

After I completed my M. Tech with petroleum refining as specialization, I got an interview call from an American Oil company in India whose parent company in USA, later merged with another Oil Giant and now is world largest oil company. I negotiated for some increments and higher salary for my post graduation qualification. But, Director – Technical, rejected my request saying "I need to justify my merit by my performance in job, but not by mere qualification". The American Oil company had a housing policy to give their officers accommodation in their officers' colony. As it is difficult to get housing in Bombay, my parents advised me to take up the job in National Petroleum corporation Ltd. the two American oil companies after nationalization). Few Indian companies could boast of a residential colony with bungalows, swimming pool, club house, Tennis courts for officers. Thus I joined my dream job with part of Bungalow sharing with my colleagues and over looking a spacious lawn which is a bigger dream. As my dream has come true, things were not all that cozy at recruitment level. One of my school mates who did his Masters in science was taken as Technician. Then there another govt. policy to recruit graduates from reservation category, where merit is not main criterion. Then some children of employees were given reference. In short, recruitment was tough and different in private and public sector companies. I some how got the job in merit category. As employment was tough those days, merit continued to be criterion on paper, while recommendations continued though back door. Thus there was gradual deterioration started in recruitment due to job reservations and recommendations.

Old Caltex

Three Management styles

Management style is situational. It varies with men, material and resources. It may not be prudent to compare different styles of management, I say, what works is management as the maxim goes "proof of pudding lies in eating." During my stay in Indian oil company, I came across 3 senior executives

George, Nariman and Prasad (names changed to keep their privacy). First two represented American management style, while the last one came from public sector. All three had different styles and in general worked well, except that none of them could stop the attrition of qualified man power and limited growth of the company due to limited resources. Leaders are admired for their problem solving ability more than any other quality. Successful managers in India rank high in retaining talent as till recently many corporations had very limited resources. Let us see how three Leaders handled the oil company while it was Indianized.

Fire fighter from the front

George was a hard working science graduate worked his way to top during American management. He studied all the design manuals and was able to discuss in detail the technical details. His ingenuity resulted in a lot of saving for refinery. one example was while other rival oil companies were spending Rs 400 crores for a similar project, he lead a team to complete 2 million Tons crude processing expansion project in Rs 80 crores (almost USD 50 Million) well within the budget. Government of India which was in socialistic pattern had a peculiar way of rewarding oil companies by giving 12% return on investment. So those who spent 200% extra cost of project were wrongly rewarded for cost over-run and time over run. This is an example showing, how Public sector units do not having Economic consideration.

George used to be the first person reporting to duty and last person to leave the office, daily. When there was big tank fire, in spite of being a Director, George fought the fire from the front. He was a role model for many and yet was denied Chairman post as he arrived late for the CEO interview. There was rumor that Promotions in Public sector are fixed based on their proximity to power and not always merit. Thus a hero in the eyes of many, could not secure a top post. This is an example, how succession is planned. CEO post was finally filled by a charted accountant, who looked at complex refinery and marketing as a commercial unit. Many public sector units, are run by bureaucrats and IAS officers who allocated resources and monitored PSU like government offices.

Gordon was surprised how a director who completed his project at half the budgeted cost was ignored for promotion.

The perfect Leader

Nariman(name changed) was a *Parsi* (an ethnic group from Iran who took refuse in India after Islamic invasion) gentleman known for his self confidence, self respect and empowering his staff. He was a good executioner and was a role model for youngsters like me at that time.. He also rose from the ranks and used to be different from George in some respects. While Nariman was comfortable in delegating the work, George was comfortable in 100% control of affairs. Nariman never stayed after 4 PM in the refinery and believed in Empowerment while George was a late sitter in the office and a perfect back-seat driver. Nariman's instructions were typical of 100% empowerment. He used to say "call me only if refinery is on fire". Under him, staff felt the responsibility. While, George was a typical Indian benevolent leader, Nariman was molded in American style. Nariman was known for his punctuality which was legendary. Not surprisingly, many used to admire Nariman and he followed American management style. The conflict between George, who was director and Nariman, who was General Manager was interesting to watch. But both worked in tandem and refinery and oil company were at its best till the third person "Prasad" took over.

Horses may run away

Mr Jitendra Prasad (name changed) was our General Manager, who joined our oil company hired from a public sector company. Prasad was a science graduate and was promoted to be General Manager. One day he went to Delhi to interview bright engineers for our company. I received a fax from him asking me to send list of questions to Delhi. I promptly sent them. Immediately I received a return fax "where are the answers?". I sent the answers also. After returning from Delhi, General Manager triumphantly declared" I interviewed many young bright engineers and I selected some above average but enthusiastic engineers".

I was about to ask him" why not brightest". He continued, nonchalantly," if we hire horses, they may run away. But donkeys will stay. Hearing this, I decided not to stay longer in the company and I thought I am a thorough bred horse. Public sectors due to their recruiting policy with reservations and recommendations slowly reduced to mediocracy than meritocracy. While in promotions also seniority slowly was a consideration and mediocracy became a norm and not accepting it as the reason for attrition is real problem after nationalization of American company.

Prasad had management style which did not infuse confidence in his staff nor he delegated the work. He was a perfect example of micro management and always used to say " it is like having a snake in the bed to have Hydrogen plant in the refinery". He wanted to know hour-by-hour health of the plant nor developed staff. However, he was a best rated by his bosses as he followed their instruction and implemented them meticulously which of course resulted in good production and inventory. As a result, development of leadership suffered and what followed Prasad was mediocre management and "Yes men" to Head quarters. It was a typical back-seat driving from central government, which took away freedom and controlled PSU (public sector Undertakings) from Delhi.

Succession plan

Federal Government had a bureaucratic approach to factories which is one of the biggest drawbacks of economic progress. Fortunately some public sectors like nuclear and space organizations, where merit alone was consideration did not suffer as much as Oil companies and Banks. Human resources was the first effected department where administration became less transparent and less flexible unlike during American management.

Appointment of CEO by ministry of Petroleum has only added to problems than solve them. Same was the fate of other two oil companies which were nationalized.

Transparency and Talent recognition were the first causality

With the recruitment of mediocre talent and introducing PSU norms, troubles started in American Oil company. There used to be a sign board behind me on the wall in my office "We will take up impossible tasks Today and leave miracles for Tomorrow". That was the motto of the American Oil company. Officers took pride in their work, every body talked about new ideas and there used to be a lot of enthusiasm in the work place. Nationalization has seriously affected two most conspicuous qualities of the American Oil company. One was employees were earlier free and open to come up with their ideas, suggestions and feed back on management decisions. After nationalization, new ideas were not encouraged and lack of fairness and Transparency marked the PSU working style. It is not common to see PSUs trying new technologies nor generate patents. Here is a classic example, how an idea to use new technology was not encouraged in the newly nationalized Oil company.

Fresh from IIT, I was enthusiastic to bring in the Technology push to my company. I referred many technical journals and came out with a proposal to replace "phenol" which was toxic and not safe for operator handling. The report recommended state-of the-art technology. Though it involved additional cost, it would improve yields as well as safe to handle. Once I released the report, my senior manager sent the report to chief manager, he in turn sent it to General Manager operations who finally sent it to director. Director nominated a team to study the same who visited USA, japan and Europe and finally came with same conclusion as my report. There was a tug of war between Director and GM who should take the credit for the report. Director wanted the team to get credit while GM supported my report. I came to know of this tussle when my manager asked me the date, we submitted the report. Soon it was clear, no body wants to encourage the talent and Transparency became first causality in the public sector. As a result, a host of issues like Recognizing talent, giving credit to the intellectual property, accepting the mistakes, lack of systems and procedures to tap the ideas and harnessing them for the betterment of company all suffered. That is one of the main reasons for brain drain from India to America in 1970-90's. *While India produced best engineers from IITs, most of them did not stay in India and majority went for further studies in USA and settled there for better salaries and better recognition.*

Fixing the people instead of problem: Another example of lack of Transparency was not fixing the problem but fixing people. In a new project where an engineering error occurred while 15 mm was supposed to be the weir height, it was erroneously taken as 51 mm which increased solvent ratio by 80% and increased the operating cost to vaporize the solvent. After shutdown, it was found out and instead of rewarding the engineer who pointed out the fault, project group tried to hush it up and promoted the manager who did the mistake. This lack of Transparency and fairness is blatant and typical bureaucratic way, no body raised the voice against it. I understand some senior people had to pay the price for raising the issue and the mistakes were brushed under the carpet. This speaks volumes of lack of Transparency in public sector as well as in many public places India. Failure of contractor or collapse of a fly over are under investigation for decades and culprit is rarely booked.

Brain Drain and Exodus?

If resignations are any indications for discontent in the company, attrition was 20% per year in Technical Department, where I worked, which was very high by any standard. some middle management officers got offers from oil companies in Singapore and Middle East and exodus never stopped. Added to it senior management started giving excuse, that if more people leave the company, remaining will get better chances for promotion. Many youngsters bought this logic, though experience and skill were the biggest loss, as no body cared. It is the fate of many Public Sector undertakings, with few exceptions. If Employees are not taken care by the corporation, its rivals will sure take care of them. Employee recognition is most important pre-requisite for any successful Enterprise.

Employee talent recognition

- Appreciation
- Advancement
- Empowerment
- Recognition

Em(pty) power !

If not promoted, a star performer will be hired by your competitor

Following the Rule -Book: most of the public sector units like the present Indian petroleum corporation followed rules broadly as laid down by environment and safety, if not on Succession and Empowerment. *What was missing is the risk taking capacity and Entrepreneurship.*

In Indian public sector, or for that matter in scams, it is the small fish which is caught not the big fish. I recall one incident, one officer was caught in using a wrong travel claim quoting some body else's ticket. He claimed reimbursement of first class ticket expenses, which he did not travel. As his bad luck would have it, a Bishop in the church, who originally travelled on the ticket gave his witness against Mr. Mahammad. (name changed). As he was a leader in officer's association, it is rumored that management victimized him. Later a bigger scandal came to light, involving oil pilferage on daily shipment of tank trucks, where some of innocent people were victimized. As it is difficult to prove, the case was closed limiting the damage to few officers who admitted their crime. Thus following rule book is limited to few lower level staff in public sector. Big fish in the scam who were named during interrogation were never questioned.

Future of Oil companies and Lessons learnt: Gordon was a little disappointed with my story. It seemed, he must have preferred to have summary of differences between American and Indian Management, including cultural differences. In fact, he wanted to know what conditions prompted Indian Mangers to evolve their style. I explained to Gordon, nationalization deprived the oil company of crude source,the basic raw material, which was not in abundance in India. Though security consideration was main reason for nationalization of oil industry, lack of Crude and finances made the decision, a dead horse till the policy was reversed almost 30 years after when two private companies were given license to start Petroleum Refineries. Coming from a country, where not only Oil industry but majority of industries are in Private sector, Gordon, wanted to know the l problems faced by Public sector Undertaking As summarized by *Ms Vidya Sethi*. (Reference no. 6) they are:

- Regulatory Procedure and Related Delays:

- Unnecessary Control:

- Inadequate Diversification:

- Reservation for the Small Sector:

- Lack of Finance and Credit:

- Low Ratio of Profit:

Author's Note: Exceptions to this rule exist such as ISRO (Indian Space Organization) and DOA (Department of Atomic energy).

6

SURVIVAL STARTEGIES OF LICENSE AND PERMIT RAJ

> *Learning is not compulsory... neither is survival.*
>
> *– W. Edwards Deming*

WHAT CONDITONS PROMPTED INDIAN MANGERS TO EVOLVE THEIR STYLE?

After I narrated my own experience at a Public Sector company in the oil sector, Gordon was wondering, how other Indian corporations were performing. I told him there are industry conglomerates like TATA Sons who have USD 100 Billion empire started some time in 19th century by a Parsi family. The company grew globally from USD 400 Million assets since 1991, thanks to Economic reforms introduced by Government of India. TATAs have employees larger in number than combined Employees of Microsoft, Apple, Boeing, IBM and Google. Many private companies grew in terms of assets, no. of staff as well as market capitalization. TCS, Infosys and many more IT companies are listed in New York stock market. These companies followed the four principles of Transparency, Succession, Empowerment and Rule-book. However, many more companies in India were street smart and learnt their own style of management based on conditions prevailing prior to Economic reforms in 1991. While I am making a distinction of prior to reforms and after reformers, few conditions and few corporations still exist and function exactly same way prior to 1991. Some are wise and they implemented sound principles early and some became wise afterwards. But what conditions prevailed prior to 1991 are listed here, which prompted Indian management style to evolve their own strategy. Some principles never change like some principled human beings choose to keep up their value system while some compromise with people and compromise based on circumstances. License and permit Raj prior to 1991, has prompted many companies to adopt survival strategies and some are listed below. One of the great quality of Indians is adaptability and adjustment to situations which is one reason why they survived 1000 years of foreign rule.

India is not just a subcontinent, but a mini world

Now there are many websites and books giving their view of on Indian style of Management. One has to bear in mind, any generalization has its limitation. India being a subcontinent, is a world of its own. From North to South, East to West, apart from languages, GDP of Indian states also vary from ratio of 1 to 10. while western Indian states like Maharashtra and Gujarat and Northern Indian states Haryana and Punjab compare well with developed economies, north east is almost like Tibet and Bhutan. Southern Indian states have population with high education but risk averse attitude. Where as, *Gujaratis* (another state in western India where Prime Minister Modi comes from) are traditionally traders doing business not only in India but in Africa, Europe and Americas. Richest Diamond merchants in the world are Indian and virtually world Diamond trade is in the hands of few *Gujaratis* since centuries. Many Indian Enterprises follow age old Indian culture which one may classify as Indian management style. Some Indian traits are centuries old while some traditions were acquired during 1000 years of foreign rule. Some are limited to only cities and some are followed by educated Indians who are white collared employees. There are pockets of Indian societies who follow 20th century traditions. That does not stop young graduates from IITs(Indian Institute of Technology) who straight away fly to USA and few of them occupy the top positions as CEOs in multinational companies and few names like **Satyam Nadella** Of Microsoft and **Pitchai** of Google are known all over world. Thus any generalization about India gives a distorted picture to west as few still looked at snake charmers, while others looked at ISRO (Indian space organization) which sent 108 satellites into space on a single day. India is not a subcontinent as many describe it, it is a mini world. It has all the religions of the world and civilization as old as Syrian Christians, Iranian origin Paris fled from Iran during Islamic period, to the latest Dalia lama who took refuse in India during occupation of Tibet by China. If you look at Indian cross section not just all religions, economic strata of super rich, rich, poor, below poverty starving people to middle class all exist. In just middle class which is larger than Population of Europe has upper, lower and elite class (with assets but no cash) live peacefully. If you look at some Indian traits and conditions which prompted street smart Managers to evolve their own style to cope up with License & Permit Raj which lasted till 1991. It is interesting to know some general traits of Indian business leaders prior to economic reforms.

Four Broad areas

While each corporation and each individual is different, for centuries, Indians are known as traders to the world, who travelled by silk road or by sea route. Indian universities were at one time the best in the world. Educational superiority of India lasted till *Allauddin Khilji* destroyed *Nalanda* University in 11th century and destroyed 9 million books. Manufacturing superiority lasted till British broke the back bone of textile workers. Ever since, Indians were under foreign rule and mastered the art of survival by adjustment and adopting to situations. The adjustment and adaptation can be broadly classified into four areas. Now how Indian business men and Entrepreneurs adopted to License & Permit raj is discussed in this chapter.

1. **Planning,** including, schedule and strategy.

2. **Culture** including language, communication, relations, unity etc.

3. **Education including** Training, skills, responsibility, Accountability.

4. **Managing people and partnerships** including Hierarchy, freedom of expression, Self respect, respecting and following rules, joint ventures.

6.1 PLANNING

It is difficult to plan in India due to uncertainties. For example, unreliable public transportation compelled many poor and middle class Indians to start for work much early and reach home late. It not only increased the cost of personal transport but increased number of two wheelers on the road for which city roads were not designed. Government policy changes force businessmen change their plans often. Till 1980, India allowed only 2 manufacturers to build automobiles. Later one more manufacturer Suziki was allowed to manufacture four wheelers in India. Additionally, lack of resources often force people to postpone their purchases or delay the payments or both. In my own experience, I saw a mega project of USD 2 Billion was delayed due to shortage funds to the tune of Rs 2000 crores (USD 500 Million). Hence planning becomes a big task with changing scenario of resource availability, including Time delays.

6.1.1 Time management

Street smart Indian Mangers are flexible in scheduling meetings and managing Time. While American Managers expect the schedule to be holy, Indian Managers keep schedule to suit the availability, ability and efficiency of staff as well as resources. In fact, to start a meeting without the presence of a top dignitary is considered not only insulting to him, but some times counter productive as the person instead of being apologetic, would think, we are NOT interested in business. However, different policy is applied in different places. Some successful managers in India are more strict but more patient when staff explain why they were late. Those who deal with Indian businessmen have to keep this maxim in their mind. *Time is not holy, but holy are the people.*

For Indians, family is their top priority. It is common to find key people In the office to attend emergency situations in their family. We have two options to reschedule the meeting or wait till the key person arrives. *One has to remember, Impatience is not an acceptable quality for Indian managers.*

6.1.2 Priorities or plate is full?

Another important point successful managers to remember is when a person is late for his appointment or schedule, please check if he is clear regarding his priorities. Even highest ranking officer is bogged down by low priority jobs as a famous line in kids cartoon paw patrol *"There is no puppy small, nor no job is big"*. Many executives have their plates full. It is not customary for Indian managers to say "their plate is full" and they keep accepting jobs and work. There are two aspects of this accepting jobs more than what they can handle. One it is they respect the person who entrusts the jobs to them and hence accept work though their plate is full. Second aspect is, it is considered as negative communication, if staff do not accept assignment or explain reasons for it. Simply "talk back", is not acceptable. Either case, it is not uncommon to see good and efficient staff to have their plate full. Hence delay is normal and is accepted by their bosses accepting the slogan *"delaying is understandable, but not denying" whether it is justice or work.*

Successful mangers make a check list of priority to quickly decide their action.

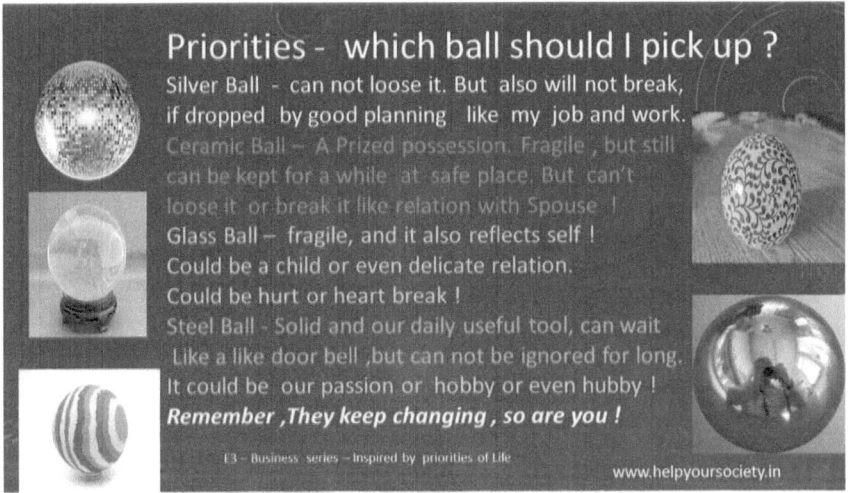

6.1.3 Plan A/plan B

It goes without saying, that Schedule of projects will be in line with Time and resource Management. **So all Indian Leaders will have Plan A/Plan B/ Contingency plan and finally re-schedule or revised plans if required.** It is an accepted practice to reschedule meetings, projects and to re-re-schedule. That is how smart executives plan in India with Plan A/Plan B and some times Plan C, D the list grows with uncertainty. *The flexibility and resilience of Indian managers is legendary.*

6.2 CULTURE, LANGUAGE AND RELATIONS

During foreign rule which lasted 1000 years, the biggest causality was freedom of speech and thus communication is skewed in India. Even after independence, communication continued to flow from top to bottom. Hence silence can not be taken as agreement, but often it is disagreement. After British rule, English was accepted as official language. Earlier unifying language Sanskrit was replaced by English. As Hindi is not accepted as a link language by south Indians, unifying factor is religion or unified Bharat, a concept established by ancient sages of India. During independence struggle, it acted as a unifying factor. Now after independence, it is no more a unifying factor and in 75 years, there were not enough efforts to improve patriotism among citizens except during war and crisis. Patriotism is not a big draw and Indians are truly global citizens as they are largest ethnic community in many countries. Thus Indian culture is still a big unifying factor. With thousands of years of Indians history and culture, it is very strong. Though English is widely used, it is not uncommon for different regional language groups coming together to speak in their language for easy communication. Thus regionalism is a binding factor as well as dividing factor.

Another important factor, one has to remember is that Indians are emotional as they work through their heart. Hence relations are very important in India. Family relations are more important and work relations play crucial role in professional commitments. *Successful managers have understood Indian communication which is not open and it is top down.*

6.2.1 Openness in communication

One common feature in American and Indian management is high importance given to communication. Probably in democracy, communication is most important tool. However, while American communication is direct and Transparent, Indian communication any thing but transparent. Both countries have high pitch of moral preaching and high ethical values as shared. In India, the communication is one way while in America, it is Two-way communication.

While transparency is not a thing which Indian managers or employees can boast off, few aspects of communication as feed-back and negative feed back, and top down communication are covered below.

6.2.2 Top-down communication

Majority of the corporate communication is top-down communication, it is like water which flows from top to bottom. Most of the times, it is monologue from the boss and few interruptions and fewer questions asked. Of course, some successful mangers are asking for feed-back, though they are not majority.

6.2.3 Communication – feed back

It is customary for an American Manager to end his address or communication with a customary tag line " any questions pl.?". But it is customary for Indian staff not to ask questions, even if the boss asks for feed-back. Not only Indian Managers do not expect any questions, but also assume staff have no questions to ask. Of course, exceptions are there in IT sector and academic institutions.

It reminds me an anecdote how Mr. Gorbachev managed approval of *Politburo* (Political Bureau of the Central Committee of the Communist Party of the Soviet Union), for dissolving themselves(Politburo) during the famous "Perestroika" and "Glasnost". A similar thing happened in India under Prime Minister PV Narasimha rao who obtained approval from his cabinet for his Economic reforms in 1991. When some one had a doubt if the proposal would go though smoothly, Rao narrated discussion between Gorbachev and his assistant. The question was "if Politburo does not approve its own dissolution, what is the alternative?". It seems Gorbachev replied" There is no word called "disapprove" in the dictionary of *politburo*. If required, we will tell them, "no approval" is NOT an option. This gives an idea of communication in many Indian corporations.

Many times, CEOs will go on monologues and some board members complete their entire career without opening their voice. NO wonder several board members do not know about shell companies and syphoning of funds which prompted in 2014, Modi Government to suspend 200,00 directors and cancel registration of equal no. of companies for not following Rule-Book.

One –way communication –
A common feature
in Indian Management style

6.2.4 Negative Feed back a big "No"

In 1998, I was to join largest private company in India at a senior position. I asked their HR head, "when so many qualified engineers were available in India, why I was invited for the interview from abroad". I got the reply "Indian executives do not want to give negative feed back to their bosses. Some times, bosses do not want to hear the bad news, some times staff do not want to give the feed back which reflect on their performance or perception.", As there is a tendency to push the problems under carpet, we hire some senior people from abroad. A similar thing happened to my project Director who had to leave the project, as he gave a realistic picture of the project. When funds were not available, the project was delayed, Gordon, in spite of my caution gave a realistic picture to the owners and as a result, the Family owned Business house took a decision to sack Gordon to protect the image of the company. A negative feed back is not encouraged by Indian business leaders as it spreads despair and disappointment and dampens the spirit of team. One can also assume, it may create negative impact on public image and which affect credit worthiness and hence avoided. But no body even raises the issue of "Transparency" in many family run Business houses.

6.2.5 Meetings, interruptions

we can expect meetings to start on time at few occasions. But mostly meeting starts when top boss enters the meeting and ends when he leaves. We can expect interruptions as per hierarchy. A top man can stop or prolong a meeting and as per his wish can interrupt the meetings. But the same freedom is not available for others. It is not uncommon to see meeting gets being re-scheduled. Again it is as per convenience of top boss, not others. Some times meetings continue for hours or even days. So those who are new to Indian meetings, have to learn to keep spare time available for re-schedules. Many times, the agenda of the meeting is stretchable or flexible. Few people often monopolize the proceedings and few object to it. It is a disrespect to cut short a long speech or extempore speech or emotional outburst.

I recall one incident, in the American Oil company which was nationlaised, there was a General manager who still followed old style of conducting meetings. At the specified time, he and me were only present in the meeting room. He looked at his watch and informed me that meeting is over and asked me to stay back and inform others who come late to the meeting. Of course, those cases are rare and leaders are as extinct as dinosaur in the board rooms.

6.2.6 Relations vs Results

What is unique about India is here relations are more important than results. In America, relations are built on results. That makes a lot of difference as many employees would like to work long term with the companies, if not, for a life time as in japan. However, the short time, result oriented American culture is not well received in India. We also observe, in teams, we do not see direct criticism, but even if negative feed back has to be given, it need to be given in private. *"Praise in Public and reprimand in private"* is the accepted practice. As it was discussed earlier, it is a Ring-road approach or round about way of communication. But main point is Relations have to be maintained in India, irrespective of results or real feelings. If we compare with Middle East, India is better, where Arabs maintain protocol and relations and formal relations irrespective of even enmity. In India, Relations brig results, while in west, results bring in relations. So also in India, ***Relations do not come without strings, relation means taking higher responsibility***. So team work is given more importance in Indian corporate sector. India is a community oriented society unlike west which is Individualistic society.

6.2.7 Family first

No body should underestimate the value of family in one's life in India. Successful Managers never forget to enquire about family first before going to details of work related issues, at least with senior staff. Also those who care for the family issues, will get the loyalty of staff. There is a story about a driver who got treatment in America spending millions of dollars and that incident influenced the entire NTPC corporation and many HR experts highlighted that issue as a role model for corporate governance. It is common for successful Indian mangers to accept family related excuses for late arrival to office and delayed project delivery in special cases. "Family comes first" is a mantra all Indian mangers have to remember always!

6.3 EDUCATION AND TRAINING

Education is given highest priority in India, since ages. Indian government gives free education and made it compulsory also. However Training has taken a back seat. Recent education changes and reservations for certain groups irrespective of lack of merit put a question mark on quality of education. Then responsibility and Accountability are not part of education curriculum. Prolonged foreign rule has set a wrong trend in defying laws and also skirting responsibility. Democracy and appeasement has added the problem of lack of Accountability.

6.3.1 Training and coaching

For a strange reason, British education and English knowledge is still considered substitute for Experience in India. Probably British took graduates as IAS officers and they learnt on the job or British education produced clerks and collectors to document and collect taxes. The result is that age old craftsmanship in India is not respected any more. In fact, dignity of labor is low in India compared to many western countries. As a result, work or skill are not developed. In fact, Training is viewed by many as an inferior assignment and management also considers it as time waste. Many considered Training as paid leave or a perk at 5 star hotel and that concept is continued. What ever one has to learn in the school is also limited to memorizing books and many consider it "bookish knowledge". Thus Training is taken a second seat compared to education, where as both are like two wings of a bird which are equally important.

It is not uncommon to see a mechanical engineer who do not dare to open a bonnet of his automobile or a civil engineer to take up a job in Information Technology. Skill in their own filed is not given importance by students nor employers. In fact, IQ and written tests are given higher weightage while recruiting, instead of their core professional competence. This is the result of British rule which continued even after independence, when they focused on Administration than Accomplishment. Even now, knowledge of English and report writing are considered more important than on the job training.

Note: There is a big drive by the present government under "Skill development" scheme, to increase employability of various students who have completed their education without much application.

6.3.2 Lack of learning habits and reading books

It is my personal observation, in comparison to no. of educated people in India, no. of books published are far less. Government provides low cost text books and no need for students to purchase text books. For Many Indians, learning stops after completing schooling. We do not see a big enthusiasm to learn new habits and management theories which slows down progress. Based on a large pool of scientists and Engineers in India, the no. of scientific publication in reputed international journals is dismal. However, lack of reading habit is compensated by internet and kindle as India became 2nd largest user of Internet and digital data recently, in 2019.

6.3.3 Coaching

Some successful mangers consider coaching as part of their job, But mostly training is given lower priority due to lack of funds. In fact, there are mentors in every section of India. If you loose your path or looking for directions, In America, we do not find any one to guide us except sign boards. In contrast in India, no one goes by sign boards but at every corner, you have enthusiastic public who are ready to guide us or who take pleasure in advising us voluntarily. It is considered a good act to advise and coach. That makes easy for learners though few find it un solicited interference. In short, successful mangers in India do not loose the opportunity to coach.

6.3.4 Responsibility and Accountability

Hukuna Matata.(a catch word used in the famous cartoon picture The Lion King) No Roles, no responsibility and. No worry.

When credit is not given to the efforts, intelligence and integrity, it is not just employees, no body acts with responsibility. When top has no integrity, there is no way he/she can fix accountability. When your stakes are zero in profits or progress, why bother about results? This sums up average Indian mind. Only way to change it is by Inspiration, Not by motivation.

The 2 key things missing in employees are 1. responsibility 2. Accountability. Two key things missing from Indian management are 1. Empowerment 2. Succession plan.

Responsibility: Though we covered "Responsibility" in the previous chapters as it is a wide spread, I find it is necessary to explain how few successful managers handled it. Lack of freedom is one reason, why so many people refrain from taking responsibility. It is like a child who thinks attending school and learning good habits is for the sake of their parents. On the contrary, over possessive parents guide children and some times, it is difficult for children to act independently. Another peculiar habit we find in India is while few people take up responsibility and fewer educated people take up social responsibility in India. It is strange, many keep their homes clean, but leave the road and their neighborhood. A similar attitude is found in departments, They take care of their section, but not bothered about its impact on other sections and departments. Hence many CEOs take extra responsibility and make sure every thing is right which resulted in micro management. Coupled with blame game, lack of responsibility, Micro management has become essential to over come not only external threats, but internal inefficiency. Till economic reforms were introduced, lack of resources for employers, lack of appreciation for employees did not produce responsibility. However, some sections of society are highly responsible, who progressed very well and quickly too. Indian government has IAS(Indians Administrative service), who are back bone of executing government polices and are considered responsible for progress of India.

Accountability: Though both Responsibility and Accountability are related, there is a need to mention about Accountability, till as late as 2014, not many company heads were booked for fraud. Even bureaucrats have associations and courts protect individual rights which are mostly misused by individuals to protect themselves under pretext of exploitation of management or government.

Even share market till digitization was implemented in 1991, was manipulated by many business tycoons and stock brokers alike escaping accountability to shareholders. Same hold good for employees also, especially in government sectors. Thus only few weak and lower rung employees were tried for accountability. Biggest escape was by political leaders who amassed wealth without any fear of punishment.

6.3.5.Comradeship Paradox

The fact that India is a land of paradox has to be borne in mind always. While team spirit is not one quality, Indians can boast, comradeship is not lacking. What does it mean is at lower level of performance, job protection is prevalent But at high level of performance, competition is high. The great Indian crab story I narrated earlier is regarding job progress. In short, the lower level jobs, we see a very high level of comradeship to cover up to hide the mistakes; where as at board level, we see a back baiting and discounting of achievements in private, but silence or appreciation in public. Another Indian peculiarity is those who are successful would like to share their success with all and those who failed look for excuses. In other words, accountability is missing, so is credit for Victory. It is an accepted practice for bosses to claim credit for their achievements while discredit is pushed to staff.

6.4 MANAGING PEOPLE AND PARTNERSHIPS

Managing people in India has to be understood in the back ground of strong leaders and self respecting individuals. Also trust which is generally lacking is reflected in games people play in joint ventures and ideas, patents etc. in a society innovation is highly visible trait, patents are low due to the fear of copying and plagiarism. Lack of strong rules and lack of enthusiasm of implementing rules and wide spread corruption are cited reasons for it.

6.4.1.Strong Individuals and Benevolent dictators

Another paradox in Indian leadership is that till you reach the top position, a strong man is viewed with suspicion by the top leaders. But once you reach the top, unless you are a strong individual, it is difficult to survive as lack of team spirit and lack of unity puts a lot of pressure on leaders to take wrong decisions. If a leader is already popular or accepted by all, his popularity gives him choice to decide. Till then, one of the political moves by all and sundry is to select weak leader so that he will listen to the coterie.

The paradox is that every body wants strong leaders and strong leaders are eliminated on their way to top positions. Many corporate leaders eliminate any one who raises questions, shows individualism or strong views in the beginning. That is one of the reasons why many staff never give their opinion or feed back which displeases bosses.

6.4.2 Benevolent dictators

Patriarchal society in India has produced benevolent dictators who enjoyed a lot of support in both politics and Business establishments. Gandhi, who is considered by many as father of modern India, did insist on eradicating untouchability and supported reservation in jobs for certain back ward classes.

It augurs well with a tolerant society of India. obviously, performance is not the first criterion in allocating jobs. Many perform to best of their abilities, but do not like strict rules and strong punitive actions. Even if credit is denied to an employee, employees would not complain. But employees do not want to be blamed, even if a grave mistake is committed. Forgiving is considered a great quality of a leader. Even if Leader is a dictator, it is acceptable, but benevolent dictator is preferred by many. That does not mean, they accept failure of their leader. Another aspect of mas adulation is that, the stronger the leader is supported, sharper would be the criticism, if he fails. Cricket stars who are considered demi-Gods, were gheraoed at airports after their defeat in world cup. *High performance of a leader and low performance of staff is an accepted norm.*

6.4.3 Hierarchy

In the management ladder, hierarchy is maintained. Leader is NOT one among equals. Strictly Boss is above all. Not only in communication and addressing him as "Boss", but following his orders and directions is considered a "must". American Management is more flat while Indian management has more layers of hierarchy, some times, unsurmountable for many. It is a British legacy to call boss as "Sir" unlike in America, where boss is first among equals. Body language, and even language of staff shows the hierarchy. One has to observe the body language in meetings and remember Indians follow the protocol like British.

Many MNC's tried to introduce a flatter, more egalitarian structure to their Indian subsidiary in order to align it with other offices in the group. This may prove difficult in a country where hierarchy is unquestioningly accepted. One reason many explain the hierarchy is strong as India is a caste based society, where upper castes, lower castes are clearly defined. But this class difference is reflected in every area, rural vs urban, illiterate vs educated. Once a person occupies the top post, people automatically tend to respect the position.

Young generation is exception to it and gradually, hierarchy is not maintained especially in service industries. Foreigners who visit India should look for the power centers before they spend time in convincing or lobbying.

6.4.4 Self respect and Individualism:

Indians are emotional and respond with heart more often than with head.

Many Indians consider criticism as a threat to self respect. This applies to employees, workers and even street vendors. They may not answer back, but self respect and traditions are very dear to Indians which all foreigners have to remember. Some Educated Indians ridiculed uneducated and villagers and paid the price for it. "Respect all" is a safe practice any where in the world, but more so in India. It is safe not to enter into religious or caste controversies which have very high repercussions to business. For example, offering beef to a Hindu and pork to a Muslim. Mind you India has second largest Muslim population in the world. Many of them are proud that they are Indians.

6.4.5 Different Stokes for different folks

The key to successfully managing in India is understanding that your workers have different motivations than their counterparts in the United States. American workers can often be motivated with only a cash bonus, but this may not be sufficient in an Indian company. Human resources departments are important in India, so companies invest more in training, recruitment and benefits. You may need to combine fringe benefits and quality of life such as accommodations with a cash bonus to sufficiently motivate your team. Most important is the loyalty which staff attach to the leaders who care for the family of employees and relations to be maintained and human sensitive to problems especially disease and any deaths in the family have to considered for leave and absence.

6.4.6 Micro Management and Lack of Initiative

Higher Management often complains lack of initiative and staff often complain micro management or back-seat driving. It is uncommon to see Vague requests for action, with the expectation that staff will show the necessary level of initiative which usually end up in inaction. Staff are normally confused by vague instructions or fed up with micro Management by bosses which is a reason for lack of initiative among of staff. Another paradox is that lack of initiative is shown as a positives sign and waiting for instruction is seen as obedience.

6.4.7 Lack of joint ventures and Patents

In spite of many research institutes and large scientific community, we do not find any world beating Technologies, or patents in India. This may be due to lack of strict rule to protect intellectual property. We often see some successful Bollywood movies with a story line from Hollywood movies. Other contributing factors could be poor quality of higher education, lack of business ethics, lack of Transparency in Indian Enterprises. If Technology is given higher priority by Indian Business leaders like Japanese, Economic progress world have been faster.

Street smart but not Leadership !

STEET-SMARTNESS DOES NOT EAN RIGHT LEADERSHIP

Joint ventures: Many believe Indian companies often fail in joint ventures. Prof. V. Raghunathan in his book "Games Indians play" (Ref 6) explains one of the reasons is some businessmen look out for short time advantage rather than trying to make the venture succeed.

If you look at the way we behave in all kinds of situations — whether it involves jumping a red light or dumping our garbage in the streets — that kind of behavior can be explained by the prisoner's dilemma. I will keep my own house clean, but the streets are not my business. Since everybody thinks the same way, the public interest suffers. (*Ref. 6*)

What makes Indians companies stand apart

But if we look closer, what works in American, many not work in India, and what worked in India few hundred years before, many not work now....... Even what was the style prior to 1991 Economic reforms also do not work now. That takes us to the next chapter, where I met Gordon and story started in 2008. As the story will be unfolded in next chapter, I will conclude this chapter with one sentence. Every experience is unique, but wise would like to learn from other's experience. But at least learning form own experience is expected from all.

IT company giants like TCS, Infosys, WIPRO, Mahindra Tech (former Satyam computers) developed country markets as an economic alternative with their lower cost, but established themselves based on their capability and value added service to the customers. Like survival of the fittest theory, customer satisfaction and value addition to the product/services are key to any company.

There are some corporation who expanded multi fold and started new enterprisers, who followed the new trend and took advantage of economic reforms. Here is a story of a family business house who started with Rs 500 crores and become USD 40 Billion business empire.

PART-III

ECONOMIC REFORMS AND OPPORTUNITIES

After the conversation about Indian philosophy, some of the ideas of Quantum Physics that had seemed crazy suddenly made much more sense.

– W. Heisenberg

7

MANAGEMENT IN AN INDIAN FAMILY RUN BUSINESS

> *Success is not final, failure is not fatal: it is the courage to continue that counts.*
>
> **– Winston Churchill**

Meeting Gordon and my first impressions: In October 2007, Dubai was not very hot, winter was yet to set in. I met Gordon for the first time in Dubai in a Hotel, where he interviewed me, for a key position in a Mega project estimated at USD 5 Billion. In fact, a similar project in Kuwait, for which I came across a DFR (Design feasibility report) for USD 9 Billion here is the story where we completed the project at a fraction of the cost meeting international standards".

Gordon introduced himself as ex-project head for Foster Wheeler corporation, which is an internationally acclaimed design and construction company. Earlier in my experience with Shell International, (a US oil giant), I was familiar with Foster Wheeler and their thorough job of documentation and detailed Engineering. I was glad to know Gordon was hired as Project Director by the Indian Business house. Here again the name of the Indian business house is kept confidential to give me freedom to discuss their management practices. He enquired my back ground in Refinery Projects including projects managed by Shell International. Gordon declared his interest to hire me saying "Together we can help India build a Mega project". During our conversation, Gordon discussed details of my earlier project which had to be shelved due to economic unviability. I explained that the extra burden on project cost of new tankage and instrumentation did not justify purchase of old refineries for USD 150 million. It was an ambitious project to relocate 3 refineries from Canada to Middle East. Gordon quickly declared, "if you worked for Sharjah Refinery project, I am keen to take you in my team". It was a pleasant surprise for me, as I was about to explain why the project failed. Gordon displayed in one long sentence his breadth and width of international exposure. He said, "Mr. Campbell (my earlier project director) shared every thing about the project. It was a decision based on wrong economics. As a Head of process, your skill was on integration of 3 refineries on drawing board. My opinion is that if only old assets are revived, world refining industry would not waste trillion dollars by abandoning assets. I want you to join my group at the earliest, as we are looking for a process expert. "I realized Gordon was a visionary as his concern was waste of Trillions of dollars while many project directors look to save few thousand dollars in a project. Immediately, Gordon introduced me to the HR executive, " Raj is the best process expert. Please negotiate with him the salary and he would join us at the earliest". My first impression of Gordon was he had a great quality of a project director. He was very quick in decision making and transparent in communication.

TRASPARENCY IS THE PROBLEM

Now HR executive Mr. Varma (name changed) started negotiating with me. His first complaint was "how can Gordon appreciate you in your presence?". I concurred "yes, yes! how can he be so Transparent?". Varma continued his complaint against Gordon. His concern was that I might demand higher salary. I started my role, a benevolent leader and said "you may offer what you can afford. But after reaching India, if I come to know the offer is not comparable to the best, I may have to re-consider my decision to join". Varma knew I was serious. Gordon did not understand the discussions. I explained, "it is not customary in India, to accept subordinate's capabilities in his presence. Nor staff expect a praise from the boss, they may mistake it for a consent for a raise in salary. Same way, employees do not want be accountable for their mistakes. It is like taking a signed document absolving a doctor before a life threatening operation. This sums up transparency problem in India. Gordon was used to "Hire &Fire" and did not understand this. "If some body is good, we will hire him, if he is not performing, we will fire him," was his policy. I explained to Gordon, it does not work in India. Once you hire a person, especially a senior person, you are stuck with him and firing him will create ripples in the staff and create insecurity among them. So Indian employers are cautious in hiring and delay firing. After successful negotiation, I left Dubai. Thus my relation with an Indian family run business started. I returned to India this time to a different company where management was Indian family but wanted to implement American management policies. They hired a HR chief from a world famous American soft drink company, who took over as Head of Human Resources group. Later, I came to know STAR OIL was a part of one of the biggest group of companies of India doing various businesses ranging from shipping to Real estate.

ATTRACTING TALENT AND REWARDING LOYALTY

Family run business house knew they have to pay better salaries than Public sector, to attract talent.

One point both public sector unit staff and foreign investors have to know that Private family owned companies value loyalty to the owners. Job security is lower in private sector than in Public sector and yet very high compared to the west. Most of the Indians like to work in secure environment and those employers who provide the job security enjoy the loyalty of employees. Thus private sector had a better chance and zeal to retain and reward employees. Thus brain drain observed in public sector company was not reflected in many well established private companies. In fact, in companies like TATAs, there are employees with 3-4 generations in the service of TATA companies like Tata Steel. Though majority of private sector is a low paymaster than public sector, few sectors like Oil, and IT were pioneers in retaining and rewarding talent.

By retaining and rewarding talented Employees, private sector had a better chance to implement succession plans than PSUS. Thus continuity of operation, implementation of strategy were achieved by Successful Leadership.

Growth of the family run Business

When we look at growth of STAR group of companies, a small construction company started few decades back, with meagre investment, reached USD 40 Billion revenue in less than 2 decades. Star had several lines of business such as project management, Oil refining, real estate, IT, shipping and steel and was one of the top 10 companies in India owing its growth to Economic reforms and their Enterprising skills. STAR is a real star among Business houses as they chose Tatas as their role model. However few like STAR Steel had a high liabilities. Another aspect which is an accepted practice in India is to entrust their projects to some sister concerns of their group. This coupled with liberal loan policy of federal government and flexible share market in India benefitted innovative finance and cash policies of the family group. We were in a strange situation where our client and owner of the project and executor of the project are from same group of companies. There was a confusion for me initially, as I did not know who was the owner, who was client. Some groups had different management styles based their CEOs and their back ground. Few CEOs were hired from public sector, few from private and some from foreign multinationals. In our project group, majority worked abroad and I could see the difference in management styles and thus became the subject for my book,

What kept Star apart from other companies is that they believed in best Management practices while keeping Indian traditions, in tact. As Oil business involves lot of capital, huge cash flow and infrastructure building, STAR kept tight financial control. Those companies who did not have fiscal discipline like Birla Group, who entered into Petroleum refining a decade earlier had to retreat and opt out of Oil sector. Of course, it was a joint venture who did not have freedom nor resources leave alone management and leadership for pulling the economic miracle which others achieved almost a decade later.

Project Management and Operating company

I joined the project team initially. Same Star group has an operating company Star Oil refinery and the story begins here between Oil company and project company. Though both companies are owned by same Family house, they operated with different management styles. In tandem, one operates by international style while other operates in Indian style and vice versa making it a bitter struggle or interesting tussle as readers can imagine. Often our Managing Director used to get vexed when both project and operating groups clash. "it is my money at stake" used to be a common complaint of the Employer.

For easy reference I will call the two groups, project group and refinery group, interestingly, I worked in both groups first in the project group and then in Refinery group. Readers would remember both these groups are separate companies registered with their own directors and management while owners are same. Some interesting feature is like any family, head of the family has to some times intervene so that family unity and welfare is kept in mind.

Empowerment

While some of us in project group planned and scheduled our meetings, operating group was looking for permission to attend the meetings and setting up schedule. One day, I flew to Delhi to attend an important meeting. I met one senior vice president from operating group there. His first question was, how come Project guys are present in the meeting. That was because, Project Management was operating in American style while operating company was in Indian management style. Scheduling and planning is part of Empowerment. To make matters worse, some body answered, Gordon must have approved the visit. In the evening during dinner, Gordon met me in the guest house and greeted me, "so process group is taking care of Japanese on compressor issue. My colleague from operating group understood, Gordon empowered me to plan my work. Gordon was surprised to know Empowerment is not favored by many CEOs in India. Main reason for not empowering staff as it erodes their power and reduces control. It is customary for many to seek permission for small actions in big corporations. Thus Micro management and Back-seat driving is common in Indian corporate world. Slowly it is changing though old habits die hard.

IT companies took a big step in this direction. It is not uncommon to see youngsters taking over companies in IT companies. One example is **Nandan** *Nelankani* who succeeded Mr. Narayana Murthy in Infosys as Chairman.

Who was heading a mammoth identification program of govt. called ADHAR. (Pl. Ref. *Adhar* program which is largest data program in India). This speaks volumes of empowerment he received from Mr. Narayana Murthy Chairman of Infosys. which will be covered in Vol. 2 of Successful Management styles of India. Several companies are in the same path and yet the general reluctance in empowering staff needs to change.

Accountability vs Team work

I recall a crucial meeting, where one senior member from operating company wrongly concluded, one critical unit called "Sulfur recovery unit" was not a priority for construction group. Accordingly, the unit was scheduled last. But during the next review meeting, every body realized the fallacy and Managing Director reversed the decision, which resulted in delay of the project by 3 months, However, for reasons known to few, no one was made accountable for the mistake. While MD wanted to fix the responsibility for the person who mooted the wrong idea, there was general reluctance to own up the idea. I knew who initiated it, but by the time, my turn came to speak,, it was a pretty obvious to me, that Accountability is not normal in Indian management as no body spoke. MD asked formally, "who is responsible for this wrong decision". No body answered, which is normal in many board meetings in India. I kept quiet and a director next to me said" no body ". MD laughed and said" if no body said, How did I remember it? it is not normal to forget a thing, but difficult to remember some thing which no body said ". Every body laughed at MD's remarks and axe did not fall on the senior vice president who did the blunder".

Accountability was the causality and Team work prevailed. Covering mistakes is viewed as Team work and the leader is expected to take up the fault of the team members. He may cover it up or expose based on the relation and importance of the team member. Some times this leads to coterie and groups in the team, but that is acceptable in Indian conditions. This reminds me a big Himalayan blunder done by Nehru in 1962 war is still not owned by congress the ruling party nor opposition is able to fix it on larger than life size God figure Nehru....... Modi, is reversing some of the policies of Nehru, 70 years after independence. But it is a Taboo to de-rate Nehru and his contribution to India. That is the Indian culture and we are expected to accept the wounds without complaining about the past. A thousand years of foreign rule was tolerated by Indians without any harsh words to Muslims nor British for the loss incurred due to them, in addition to the non-violence. Tolerance and Patience are feathers in the cap for Indians. Thus definitions of Responsibility and Accountability are different in Indian context.

In the project group, I was empowered to schedule my work, trips and meetings with clients and in total responsible for my job planning and resources were provided as per my request. My counter parts had to wait for longer time and approvals for official tours and smaller decisions. Thus there was a wide difference in empowerment of project group and Operating company.

Contrast styles of Succession Plan: while Empowerment was different in project group and operating group, an interesting but opposite trend was observed in succession plan for project group and operating company. While Empowerment was not very popular in Operating company, Empowerment was a necessity and prevalent in Project group. Where as Succession plan was absent in project group. However, Operating company had an elaborate succession plan and each senior position was marked with succession plan and many of the senior staff knew the career paths of young and senior staff alike. It was heartening to see an Indian company following international standards in succession plan and Gordon had a plan for me and as a result, after successful completion of the project, I was absorbed in Technical department of operating company and was Head of Design group till I retired.

But the story is altogether different in Project Group. Gordon one day was summoned to Head office and was asked to give a realistic picture of the project. With tight budget and cost over running, project delay was un avoidable. But the project director not knowing the displeasure of owners, gave a realistic picture. That was the last I saw Gordon and project was completed, though a year late. Thus the story of Gordon ends here. A successor to Gordon was appointed without a plan and the project work continued. Then as the project ending completion, project group had many heads, many of them left quickly. It was obvious that project group had no succession plan and it showed up in the performance and future of project group. It is to operating group's credit to involve and spin off an organization called" Refinery Operation Group" who accomplished the part left by Project group. Again with no specific succession plan, project group had to be dismantled after completing the project. Thus a great opportunity is lost to gain from the experience of completing a mega project of USD 2 Billion and any company would have built a USD 10 billion empire from that project group. A contrast of experience in planning their succession is followed by Larsen and Toubro, which helped them as the largest construction company in India. L&T as it is popular, is a leading contractor for Metro railway in major cities of India. L&T was established by two Foreign contractors Larsen and Toubro in 1970s. Their success story is covered in volume 2 of "Successful management styles of India".

Skill Development

To match the size of the mega project, Star Oil stepped up staff recruitment and getting competent staff was a problem faced by us. While senior staff was hired selectively from public sector and private sector, competency of several junior staff had to be compromised. Thus training and development to keep the project schedule became a bigger task. It was solved by hiring a Harvard graduate to look after the learning requirement as Chief Learning officer. Main task of Learning center was to inspire all the staff to give high priority

Harvard Coffee club: A monthly meeting was arranged for senior executives at Bombay office to discuss many management issues including Transparency, communication, motivation. A team was set up by Harvard Graduate as chief Leaning officer who made sure, the management principles are understood and practiced by senior management. Irony is that while owners of the group are needed to follow the policies of Transparency and Rule - Book, staff can not be expected to follow. This tops-turvy approach is prevalent in many sections of Indian society where some are above rules, regulations and audit. Any corporation can earn the respect of public, govt. and share holders, if Skills are focused at working level, and principles are followed by higher management. But if principles are taught to staff instead of skills, it is NOT expected bring in results. But in all walks of life in India, preaching of values is common and practice is never questioned nor focused. Star Oil is not an exception on Transparency. Confidentiality is the excuse for not following Transparency.

Coaching and Mentoring: coaching and mentoring was a regular, daily affair and experience of senior staff was very useful. Another good feature of Star Oil is is benevolent leaders who are compassionate in training the staff. Two common characteristic traits of Indians are to focus on Education and coaching, which runs in the blood of Indians.

Development and support: An in-house Engineering design office was opened at Bombay and all the staff were supported by project group which I felt is a rare display of developing staff and first time, a group of engineers completed full off-sites and Utilities design jobs of a major refinery. It was a classic example of developing of staff. The job which was worth USD 200 Million was accomplished by in-house team, thanks to training.

RULE –BOOK: Star oil company followed rule book in all fields except finance. Though I was not responsible for fiancé, I would like to comment on one issue.

The cost over run for a project can be due to inefficiency or unforeseen emergencies. But the delay was burden on indirect cost. We have experienced cost over run and subsequent shortage of funds for the project to the tune of USD 500 million which is 25% of project cost. However innovative approach followed by project team which helped successful completion of the project.

INNOVATIVE APPROACH

While all oil companies in the would operate at profit margin of USD 3-4 dollar/barrel, star oil operated above USD 10 per barrel which speaks volumes of innovative approach in project design and operating company..

Project group has shown innovative approach in project outlay and budget. A petrochemical project was planned initially, which was dropped later due to shortage of funds. Refinery project was converted to Phase 1 and phase 2 and phase 2 was postponed. Finally as shortage of Rs 2000 crores was augmented by implementing a crude augmentation project for which we obtained funds form banks and implemented a sort of world record project for processing 2 million Tons of crude using a redundant Vacuum column for the project by selecting a tailor made crude for the project. A cost saving was achieved in Purchasing by opening an off-shore purchasing group in Dubai. Local fabricators were developed which reduced the cost of several items for the project. It was a unique feat of innovation in Oil projects. Necessity is mother of invention, but Indian penchant for completion of projects with tight budgets. For example typical ISRO(Indian space agency) budget is a fraction of NASA for a similar projects.

Innovation and Adaptation

Innovation and adaptation is an Indian trait which helped them to survive 1000 years of foreign rule. In fact, many nations under foreign rule have adopted or transformed in far less time frame. But India with thousands of years of culture and traditions, have taught the invaders a few things. Akbar the great liked the Indian mythologies and many Muslim rulers patronized temples such as Nizam. This adaptation and adjustment was used by corporations prior to Economic reforms in 1991 to deal with license and permit Raj. Few companies which are household names in India since Independence were TATAs and Birlas, Bajaj, Godrej, to name a few companies. After 1991, IT companies like TCS, Infosys, Wipro and Satyam paved the path to establish that India as destination IT services and IT service outsourcing and contributed to growth engines of India and BRIC (Brazil, Russia, India and China acronym).

8

POLICIES AND PRINCIPLES

> *It is difficult, but not impossible, to conduct strictly honest business.*
>
> *– Mahatma Gandhi*

TWO POLICIES AND FOUR PRINCIPLES

With, Economic Reforms in 1991, a stage is set for Indian corporations to compete with global companies. Few companies like TATAs, Reliance Industries Ltd and IT companies benefitted, immensely. While others took time to learn new ways to compete with best corporations, new companies from IT world learnt it fast. A second set of reforms started in 2014 under leadership of Prime Minister Modi, which are being pushed further with USD 5 Trillion as a target for Indian economy. To get the best benefit, Indian companies have to be the best corporations in the world by setting high standards.

That brings us to a point of very high importance. Having Potential is not enough, translation of capability to reality makes the difference. Of course personal and corporate policy is the key. Indian companies have been street smart and have ability to get out of any problem created by License and Permit Raj and even corrupt bureaucrats. If one is successful in India, I believe, he/she will be successful any where in the world.

Based on our observation so far, few companies are still reluctant to implement policies of Transparency, Succession plan, Empowerment and Compliance to the Rule Book. Ethics in Business is essential for success and earning the Trust of customers.

8.1.1 SMART CUSTOMERS

No doubt, a smart Entrepreneur makes profit. *But an honest entrepreneur makes the customers smart and thus customer becomes a Loyal customer.*

Ever since Apple corporation introduced Smart phone and increased its market capitalization to 1 Trillion dollars, all CEOs started looking at smart gadgets which include smart watches, smart goggles, Alexa like smart gadgets, not to talk about smart business practices and smart ideas like Uber and Electric cars, etc. But the best way is to make customers Smart is by offering best product and services. There is a general opinion among customers that commercial advertisements do not always to give product information, but attract customers towards purchasing products. This trend is changed recently by IT service companies and IT programs/Operating systems like Oracle, SAP and Block chain/Android. More recently Amazon and Microsoft have made customers smart by providing cloud services and offering savings in operating costs.

The summary of it is that in future, best corporations will not only be just Smart, but also introduce Smart gadgets and smart tools, which make customers Smart. This is the master stroke of any corporation to be best int the world.

8.1.2 BEST OFFER OF PRICE TO CUSTOMERS

If you see the Post Industrial era, companies like IBM, General Motors were the Blue chip companies with maximum market share did not stay forever as top corporation of Fortune 500. Subsequently with the advent of Internet, Dot. Com companies like AOL, Yahoo ruled the hearts of stock market. Then Microsoft, Apple, Google, Facebook, WhatsApp, Amazon, like companies who won the hearts of customers became darlings of the markets.

What does this trend suggest? **Customer is the king.**

Google followed by WhatsApp and Face-Book started a new trend which offered to customers the best prices or almost free services and are now having a last laugh at Turnover and profits. SO giving best offers to customers is the second policy which makes the future best companies of world.

The popular saying is "if we do not take care of our customers, some one else will". If we keep ourselves in the shoes of our customer and wear his glasses, world looks different. The ancient Indian wisdom says "let us all grow together". If fortune is there at the bottom of pyramid as international Managements expert *C Prahlad* said, "let us explore it". In a most populous country, if we can harness the economic power of rural folks, we already conquered 1 Billion hearts. By winning the hearts of customer, Business is sure to flourish.

8.2 THE FOUR PRINCIPLES

What are most important 4 principle? Best employee may not become best employer, In fact, best student will never become best teacher. So is an obedient child may not become best parent. So learning to work is good. But getting work done is a different ball game altogether, it is like asking a coach to win a gold medal or vice versa. *Pullela Gopichand* (most successful Indian Badminton player and coach) was all England champion in Badminton, but not a world champion. Yet he coached *PV Sindhu,*.a world champion in badminton which India produced. Not one, he coached 2 More champions from his Gopichand Academy. Gopichand knew how to become a champion. Without that he could not be a successful coach. But knowledge and execution are two different tracks. Few can travel on this parallel tracks. Gopichand knew why he lost world championship, world remembers Champions but not coaches. But champions never forget coaches. Many Indian Business leaders missed Success by not following the 4 principles. Even If you follow 3 but miss one, that will become your weak point. But if you follow all of them, success is assured. What are the 4 principles? Transparency, Successor planning, Empowerment, Following Rule Book. At one point or other, these four will become hurdles and in spite of doing every thing, fall is inevitable. Even legends failed in naming successors or struggled their entire life by not empowering and fell from grace by not following Rule book or criticized even after death by not being transparent. You may check history books or business history, only these 4 principles stand out in managing self or Business. These are called eternal values. The four principles we discussed in Chapter 3 are relevant now. While few of successful companies already implemented them and reaped the fruits, many more Indian companies are yet to realize that. That is why I suggest, Unless Transparency is established, confidence of Global Investor can not be earned. If we look at their significance,

Truth and Transparency are time tested and most powerful.

Succession plan is important to ensure continuity of the corporations lack of which was the main reason for disappearance of great empires of the world, which is applicable to any corporation.

Empowerment is what is the most important principle, so that CEOs can focus on future expansions and new business lines, acquisitions and thus grow bigger and bigger, while his present job is done by the staff whom he empowers.

Compliance to the Rule book, has become more relevant after 2008 liquidity crunch and to counter Terrorists Governments adopted financial investment route. Willful defaulters sarted syphoning public money through companies and business estabilshments. By following the Rule Book, we earn respect of public as well as government while protecting the company as well as directors from failure and deceit. At this point, it is I difficult to differentiate between a genuine failure of business and willful defaulters.

There can be many more areas in Business Management, but these four are required to make Indian corporations competing with best corporations in the world.

PRINCIPLE 1 - TRANSPERANCY is essence of earning Trust.. It can be improved by implementing 4 elements of Transparency

Transparency

4 Elements of Transparency

- Do what you say
- Document what you Say
- Record what you Do
- Review compliance of words and actions

Walk the Talk

[AUDIT]

INTELLECTUAL PROPERTY PROTECTION: one of the most important aspects of Truth and Transparency is protecting Intellectual properties. Documentation and quoting reference is an important part of Indian tradition. We have to revive our age old tradition which will bring back India the Leadership in the field of Knowledge. It will stop plagiarism which is the main problem in Today's Indian art, cinema and scientific community, especially post independence. This is one reason why with max. no. of engineers and scientists in India, number of Noble laureates dwindled from pre independent era. For India to be a Leader in Information age, protection of Patents and Copy right act is essential and need top priority." *Jugad" can never be a patent, except it can be at best an improvement, over existing patents.*

PRINCIPLE 2 - SUCESSION PLAN

"Success of a leader is not measured by his achievements, but his ability to groom a competent successor".

Leaders, who want to be immortal, have to select right successors.

One should remember, that no leader or CEO is bigger than his/her organization. Great Leaders not only have achievements, but were also successful in naming an able successor. All the effort to build up an organization is a waste, if it is left to the hands of incompetent people. Those leaders who are reluctant to hang their boots have to blame themselves for they can see their empire crumbling in front of their own eyes.

Success Plan will be successful only if all the 4 elements of Success plan are done properly. But the biggest hurdle to Succession is not implementation, but intent.

Succession plan
Succession ensures continuity of the corporation

Economic Engineering Excellence

4 Elements of Succession plan

* Identifying or selection
* Imbibing values
* Coaching

Values

↑

Principles

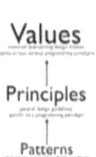

* Empowerment

Patterns

Succession is like achieving immortality of self through family !

Economic Engineering Excellence

PRINCIPLE 3 - EMPOWERMENT is essential for improving Productivity, efficiency of an organization, ease of operation as well as ensuring succession Plan.

How to improve Empowerment ?
Empowerment is to Ensure Productivity and Successful Succession plan

Economic Engineering Excellence

4 Elements of Empowerment

Training

* Training
* Developing Responsibility
* Supporting
* Ensuring Accountability

Knowledge
useful abilit...
backbone of co
quired for a tr
...day

Developing and supporting

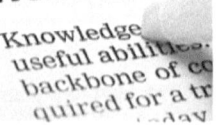

Economic Engineering Excellence

The paradox is unless Responsibility and Accountability improves, Empowerment is not possible. But unless Empowered, accountability can not be fixed. This is a catch 22 situation. Then how do we improve Accountability? Though both fixing Accountability and Empowerment are interdependent, which is one first is a million dollar question. The solution is based on the staff. Those enthusiastic take the job first and accept accountability later. Those, who are cautious, learn to be responsible first and then take up the job. It does not matter which one is first but both are essential for a successful succession plan. Accountability can be improved by developing subordinated and encouraging and regarding them for taking up responsibility

How to improve Accountability ?
Ending the Blame game is by engaging and Empowerment

4 Elements of Accountability

* Engaging employees
* Delegation of work
* Supporting
* Empowering

Engaging

It was not your fault.

Support during mistakes

Let us try to understand, why responsibility is not popular in India? As we all know, no child can grow without a responsible mother, no company can grow without responsible employees. If majority take less responsibility, remaining staff or leaders have to take higher responsibility. That is what happens in India. Like the famous 80:20 rule, if 80% do not take responsibility, remaining 20% are burdened with higher responsibility. In contrast, responsibility is taught from young age in Japan There, all school children are taught responsibility of keeping the school clean. Some families do it in India. In fact, few parents take their children's education, so serious, for few years, they shun their friends and parties. Those children fill the best schools and reach top in corporations and it is not uncommon to see some parents paly a major role in children's life. Few years back, Indian Prime Minster highlighted hygiene by declaring *"swatch Bharat"* (clean India) as national policy. This is an attempt to raise responsibility of citizens. The proof of it is now seen during "Carona virus" pandemic in the year 2020, where many Indians showed higher responsibility during Lock-out.

Successful management is fixing accountability, if responsibility is NOT taken.

Responsibility is not given; it is taken.

sri sri ravi shankar

©Polapragada SelfReliance Trust

Here is the Key to improve Responsibility and Accountability

Responsibility can not be given. it has to be taken. but Accountability has to be fixed. (given) it will not be taken. India had leaders who sacrificed their lives for independence. Citizens have to realize, it is their responsibility to elect responsible leaders.

PRINCIPLE 4 COMPLAINCE TO RULE BOOK: Those business houses like TATAs, L&T, HDFC(bank), ISRO, Infosys focused on developing responsibility among their staff. Thus their business turn over increased exponentially. Some of the blue chip companies in India showed the path to others and few became role models for the world. Some of these traits called "Indian Style" were explained by few experts (ref. 2, 11)

Compliance It is the duty and Responsibility of all individuals in a corporate Enterprise as well as in a community. For example, it is not just duty of the government to ensure discipline and traffic rules. If a community does not realize, if traffic accidents one per minute do not matter, discipline is not a matter of serious concern. Other wise, it is serious concern for the community. Compliance is a serious matter for India to prosper. A child who is brought without discipline will have freedom, but success is not guaranteed. A disciplined child can later claim freedom or independence but initially has to comply with school to complete his education. ***Thus compliance is a top priority for a successful Leader. Some times, to be role-model for this staff, some times to be role model for other leaders of the industry but, always to be patriotic and comply with rules of the government.***

Two things which can make India a super Power are

RESPONSIBILTY and ACCOUNTABILITY.

The single a thing which can take India to the top of world is

DISCIPLINE and FOLLWOWING THE RULE-BOOK,

Following the Rule-Book

4 Elements of Compliance to Rule-Book

* Systems and Procedures for Compliance
* Training
* Record of action
* Audit of Records

9

CONCLUSION AND PATH FORWARD

> *Think Big, Take Risk and Achieve Big:*
>
> *- Ratan Tata*

EVERY CRISIS IS AN OPPORTUNITY

The path forward is always towards continuous improvement; Better systems, Better procedures, Better Technology. Every Indian has to think what they have to improve in his/her own area, to make the country, a super Economic Power. The six essentials for economic progress of India rest of building on its strength.

Economic Engineering Excellence

6 essentials for progress of India into developed world

1. **Learning from past-** History – Action: Write proper history of India from AD 20 to AD 2000. including reasons why we lost to foreigners in spite of being powerful and rich nation in the world.

2. **improve Education system,** – 1000 years of foreign rule destroyed our world famous education system keep minimum standards in higher education .

3. **Improve Training skills** by improving discipline , compliance, practical application of knowledge .eg. skills like weaving and family skills to alleviate rural poverty.

4. **Develop Innovation.**- in spite of having max. number of scientists and Engineers, our inventions and patents are not upto the mark.

5. **Develop Entrepreneurship** and productivity in farming and workshops and generating money. And improve knowledge of Economics

6. **Develop systems, procedures and standards** so that quality is maintained .

Economic Reforms in 1991 was the result of a financial crisis. Post economic reforms, India had many Success stories. One of them is IT industry and Infosys is the first IT company to register in New York Stock exchange and others followed suit. TATAs have increased their turn over and Business several fold, so are many others. Reliance Industries ltd is another corporation which catapulted it self to top position post Economic reforms. While there are several reasons for it, one un denying fact is that they benefitted from Economic reforms of the Government of India which relaxed entry of private companies into Oil industry.

Carona virus is another crisis which shook the world in 2020. It is great opportunity for Indian Pharma industry which struggled to get entry into US market due to US regulations. Post Carona virus situation, pharma industry is poised to join the big league, in 2020.

How Indian corporations can be BEST in the world ?

- 1. Continue Innovation but make maintenance free gadgets and life time warrantee of services.
- 2. Create smart customers and offer best quality and price or preferably "FREE" like what's App and face book.

- 3. Accountable Social responsibility- Learn to deal with corrupt bureaucrats, Empowerment and involving rural sectors.

Responsible
Business India

- 4. Match Employee loyalty with Employer loyalty .

TRAINING

Source Book Successful Management styles of India - Author
Jayasekhar Purupogada

What Indians have to improve:

Let us review the list of items discussed in the previous chapter outlining what Indians do well.

1. Innovation:

2. Adapting and adjustment to conditions:

3. Social responsibility:

4. Employee Loyalty.

5. High priority to Education

Innovation is laudable, but many times, it is turned out to *be Jugad*, which is a make shift arrangement. While circumstances necessitated *"jugad"* (Indian word for adaptation), there are some difficulties in its acceptability by all. One problem is high cost cutting angle to it, which prevents to apply it universally with high safety standards.. If Quality aspect is introduced, "Jugad" can be improved. Same way, Adapting to situations and people is done some times to the extent, staff become sycophants forget that it is a temporary short cut and make it a standard. It is like using a short cut referable to high way.

Another aspect where most of the developing countries have to learnt to deal with deficit budgets. Subsidies given to poor are drain in their economy. More over, subsidy given by government to poorer section of society does not reach them due to inefficiency in distribution system and corruption by the middle men. While social responsibility is a laudable action, General i action on in efficiency and compassion on wrong doers is bane of society which needs correction.

Quality of education also need to be improved and in spite of third highest no. of engineers and scientists and Engineers in India, no. of noble prizes, Research papers published in international journals and patents are not comparable, leave alone the break thru technology and disrupting Technologies. There is a general feeling, government has to do some thing regarding quality of higher education. Indian Institutes of Technology and All Indian institute of medical sciences are exceptions. Recently government started accreditation of colleges and higher education which is expected to improve the situation.

Finally as we observe traffic problem and no. of accidents are high, there is general in action on safety issues except in large industries. The quality of water is another issue, while greenery and forestry divisions are taken care of Environment, compliance of pollution is still an issue.

To sum up, there is scope to improve in the areas, where Indians have traditional advantage over centuries on attitudes, but translation into results need to be focused.

Good is not enough. Great is the term described well in the famous book" Good to great "....... We want to see India to reach its pre-historic heights.......

What Indians Have to improve ?

- Adaptation - Better systems , Procedures and Technology
- Social responsibility – do not encourage inefficiency and corruption. Protect copy rights
- Employee development – Empowerment **and** Sharing profits
- Better Quality **Education and** Skill development
- Focus on Safety and Quality

Source: publishing the book - Successful Management Styles of India

Indian companies adapt to adverse situations, have innovative, cost effective **Indian style of solution often referred to as "Jugad(Indian word for adjustment)**

Several books are written on the same subject.......(Reference "Jugad" published by Penguin publishers-UK).

WHAT INDIA HAS TO DO, TO BE THE ROLE MODEL TO THE WORLD?

Their Employees have to be the BEST. Their Employers have to be the BEST. Their Leaders have to be the BEST.

BEST EMPLOYEES AND BEST EMPLOYERS

As we discussed earlier, one thing common to Employees and Employers and government in India is lack of responsibility and accountability, if all Employees think, they are Employers, Employers think, they are Employees and Political leaders think they are servants of public and public start behaving as responsible citizens, India will definitely be a role model for the world. One of the most important areas of improvement for Indians is Responsibility and Accountability.

If you are an Employee,

*   Walk to your office like an Employee

*   Work like a Team member not as an individual employee.

*   Think like the owner of the Enterprise!!

If you are the owner of a Business establishment,

*   Enter workplace, like a worker

*   Treat Employees as Partners

*   Think "out-of the Box" like an Innovator!

*   Trustee of a temple is a best goal for any Employer.

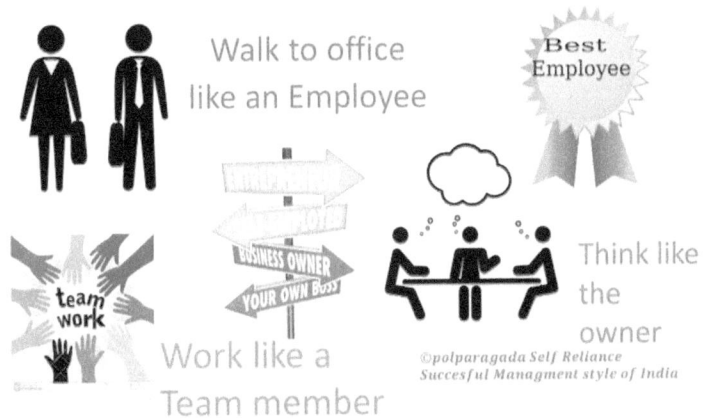

7 C's of a Successful Leader: An employee can be a Best Employee and an Employer can be the Best Employer only if puts in his best efforts. Thus Leadership is not just leading people, it is leading a committed life with commitment to principles. In fact, the greatest fall in India after independence is dearth of Leadership. That is reflected in gradual fall of acceptability of political leadership in India. Finally It resulted in Coalition governments at center. A leader requires many more qualities to be acceptable. First and foremost quality, which people look in a leader is his character. The definition of character and conduct is not easy. But perception of followers builds on "general opinion (not legal opinion) and reputation. A Leader has to fulfill his Commitment. Courage is the only quality which helps a Leader to take a step which others follow later. Without courage, a leader will be just a follower. Communication and Compassion are widely appreciated. Best way to commitment from followers is possible, If leader has the power to convey his vision to them. Leader can Compromise with people, but should never compromise on principles. A successful Leader has to have self-control which results in control on his emotions, words and actions. A leader should never forget, all the eyes will be on him, all the time. That awareness alone will make sure his conduct and character are acceptable not only to his followers, but also general public. These are 7 C's of a Successful Leader.

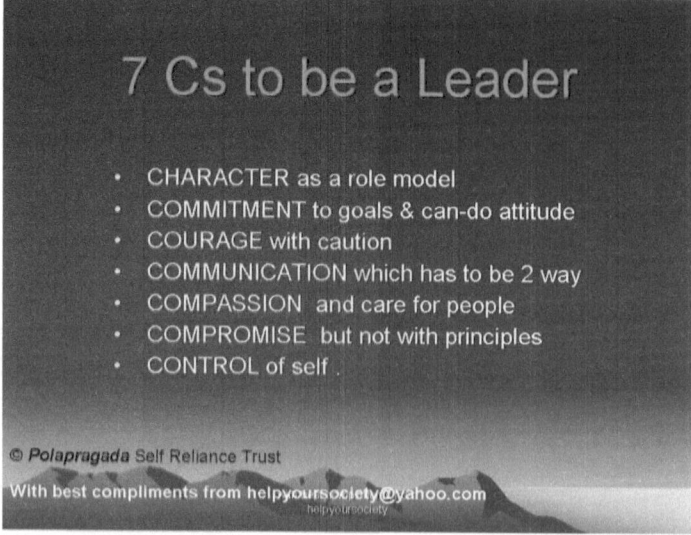

7 Cs to be a Leader

- CHARACTER as a role model
- COMMITMENT to goals & can-do attitude
- COURAGE with caution
- COMMUNICATION which has to be 2 way
- COMPASSION and care for people
- COMPROMISE but not with principles
- CONTROL of self .

© *Polapragada* Self Reliance Trust

With best compliments from helpyoursociety@yahoo.com
helpyoursociety

Good Leaders lead from the front.

Better leaders inspire than motivate!

Great leaders make their followers feel, as if they did it themselves.

Giving confidence to the next generation and preparing the successors is the biggest contribution a Leader can do to his country, company and community.

9.1 Road Map to Sustainability and Beyond

Strong, able and acceptable Leadership is required for strong and stable economy of a country or a corporation.

Here are 6 areas where India can improve which will help them to stand in the league of developed countries. Vol. 2 of the Tri series of "successful Management styles covers the subject.

Indian Business Raising

Economic reforms in 1991, created opportunities which many Indian companies shave utilized. TATAs have ventured into global acquisition and became USD 100 Dollar company. IT companies Infosys, TCS, Wipro have established India as IT power house. Pharmacy industry started in a big way and became 2nd largest bulk drug manufacture in India. Several family Houses like Reliance, Baja, ESSAR, Godrej have doubled their turn over and some even became larger and as a result India became 6th largest Economy by 2018.

Indian Business raising

- From 1947 to 1991, Indian growth rate was Hindu rate of growth between 4-5%.

- After 1991, Economic reforms by then PM PV NarasimhaRao, it shed the image of Licence and Permit Raj and growth was healthy, from a deficit forex reserves to USD 400 Billion in 2018.

- GDP grew as present day fastest economy in the world and became 5th Largest Economy USD 2.71 Trillion by 2018 (after UK, Japan, China and USA).

"**Successful Management styles** "**vol. 2** covers" How Indian companies achieved Success –(How to be Best?)

Quest to be Best

- The quest to be Best is built in for all creatures.
- Evolution theory is based on that quest.
- While Success is an indication of it,
- Many think success is survival, a handful as , sustainability.
- Rarely people realise it is self- realization.
- If any thing else is my goal, I can not be the best.
- It is True with all pursuits. it is called Passion. I call it Obsession !
- What is beyond " Sustainability ? "
- Sustainability and Beyond ! "
. Look forward to
  " Successful management styles of India – Volume 3 "

source : Book : Successful Management styles of India –
Author : Rajasekhar Polapragada

The next book of Tri series covers Future of world, Sustainability and Beyond in "**Successful Management styles**" **vol. 3**

Theory of Abundance vs Survival theory

- Survival theory assumes stronger and smarter survives.
- How ? By getting the best deal. But Survival theory is disproved by Dinosaur.
- Abundance Theory assumes , if I have a loaf of Bread, we will share half :half and work in the field together and produce wheat to make 1000 loaves of bread.
- Survival of the fittest theory assumes, we have 1 loaf and that you should get it, which makes you survive.
- If I am smart, the proof of it is making you smart.
- I want to deal with smart people or make them smarter.
- That is called fair trade and Trust worthiness.
- This the ancient Indian wisdom.
- As rishis are smarter than us, they tried to make us smarter, not survive at our cost. That is reflected in " tyage naike amrutatva manasu(sacrifice is the immortality) or meek survive the world as told by jesus.

source: Book : Successful Management styles of India : Author:
Rajasekhar Polapragada

Let all be successful, happy and peaceful!

List of References

Books/Articles/internet

1. Author: Lala Lajpat Rai, "Unhappy India", Popular Edition, (Revised & Enlarged.),1928), Banana Publishing company Calcutta 1928 https:// hindustanbooks.com/books/Unhappy_India.pdf

2. The Indian Way-By Peter Capppeli, Harbir Singh,Jitendra Singh Michael Useem, Harvard Business Press. (2011)

3. Indian reforms-BY Sanjay Baru

4. The Good Indian Guide to Queue jumping (Harper Collins,2016) by V. Raghunathan

5. The Games Indian play – we are the way we are (Penguin press 2006) by V.Raghunathan

6. Article: Problems of the Public Sector Enterprises in India By Vidya Sethi

7. Article: The 1969 bank nationalization did India more harm than good by Niranjan Rajadhyaksha is a member of the academic board of the Meghnad Desai Academy of Economics.

8. ABCD of Leadership by Rajasekhar Polapragada (2019) - Digital Edition.

9. Wikipedia – Internet data

10. IMF, World Bank reports.

11. Win-win corporations by Shashank Shah - Penguin Random House India (2016)

12. Jugaad Innovation: A Frugal and Flexible Approach to Innovation for the 21st Century by NaviRajdou et all. Published by Random House India – 2012.

13. ADHAR PROGRAM: Wikipedia

ANNEXURE 1

TEMPLE MANAGEMENT

Management styles of India-
Temple Management ©

Presentation by
Rajasekhar Polapragada- A.M.I.Ch.E
Managing director – m/s Economic Engineering Excellence L.L.P.

Economic Engineering Excellence

Management vs Leadership styles

Economic Engineering Excellence

- India was a Leading world Economy till 14th Century and successful management styles are plenty.
- Unique circumstances shaped Indian subcontinent into extreme situations where Some great Leaders had to adopt and improve Prevalent styles and some introduced new Unique management styles.
- Management and Leadership styles are dealt differently though many management gurus accepted one is Synonymous with other,
- As The canvass is vast and story is intrigue.

  I Believe, understanding India,

  is equivale to understanding the world.

  Temple Management is one Unique

  management style of India

Temple Management - uniqueness of Indian Temples

- Temples are sources of wealth in India form ages which attracted foreign invaders.
- Temples are also centres of Arts, science and Technology .
- Let us first try to understand how Temples are different from Mosques and Churches ?
- How temple management effected Indian Management styles and vice versa.?
- Let us see Origin, Ownership, Administration And finally Accountability of Management.

© ABCD of Leadership

Economic Engineering Excellence

© copy Right : Source : from the forth coming book Titled " Successful Management styles of India "

Unique features of Temple Management style

Economic Engineering Excellence

- In spite of being different ownership, Temple management have some common features.
- NO visible management
- No single chain of command.
- Ad-hockism

- Culture / Tradition
- No Accountability , full responsibility !
- Communication / Freedom
- Centres of Arts and Science.
- Voluntary contribution

© ABCD of Leadership

© copy Right : Source : from the forth coming book Titled " Successful Management styles of India "

Temple Management - Origin and Ownership

- Temples did not exist in *Krita yuga* or enlightened age. Temples are built in Treta yuga or during the time of *SriRam* (pl refer Indian Leqadership styles)
- In the beginning , there was Shiva worship and shivlingas were installed by individuals as *SriRam* also installed shivlinga in Rameshwaram.
- Later on, Vishnu Worship started when Kings built the temples and so was administration with them.
- Other temples also had committees of **Dharma kartas** (Trustees)
- Latest , govt. took over many temples and the richest Tirupati temple in Andhra Pradesh state is operated by state govt. so are many.
- Uniqueness of Indian Temples is all management styles or **ownerships** continue even today.

© ABCD of Leadership

Economic Engineering Excellence

Temple Management - Trusteeship

- Unlike Mosques and Churches, Trustees for temple are formed either on hereditary or by election or selection.
- Some temples are established by Kings and they continue to be Trustees Eg. Ananta padmanabha Swamy temple in Kerala.
- Some are taken over by govt. Eg. The famous Tirupati Balaj temple.
- Some are run by Trust eg. Dwaraka and Vishnodevi temple
- **Some are run by Archakas eg. Chidambaram and Kedarnath.**
- Some are run by public fund and management Eg. Somanath Temple
- And many more or run quasi govt. quasi priest cum Trustees and many more are run as monopolies, personal property , with confidentiality and no public knowledge of funds diversion.

© ABCD of Leadership

Economic Engineering Excellence

Temple Management – Acceptable

- Best part is No work and no responsibility for visitors.
- Acceptable to all as per Indian Tradition
- you can visit Temple of your choice
- Not compulsory except following sanctity.

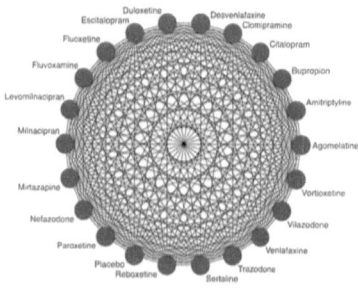

TEMPLE MANAGEMENT –
Resources – Administration

- *Many temples in North India have
  no or Nil resources due to muslim invasion.
  Hence infrastructure, cleanliness and administration is affected.
  SO also many companies in India are sick and non competitive.*
- *Some temples in South are very rich and they have Administration,
  which are doing very well,*
- *so are many IT companies in Bangalore
  who are competing with best in India.*

TEMPLE MANAGEMENT –
Fatalism and Acceptance

Jo hota hai manjure Khuda hota hai.
(*All happens as per God's will*)

- *This has both positive and Negative impact on working.*
- *No body can be blamed for what happened.*
- *Hence people are willing to participate, suggest, help, decide, determine and contribute. Ideal for group activity.*
- *However, Accountability is hard to fix .*
- *Few criticise Temple management (SACRED)*
- *Hence Acceptance of decisions IS HIGHEST IN TEMPLE.*

© ABCD of Leadership

© copy Right . Source : from the forth coming book Titled "
Successful Management styles of India "

Economic Engineering Excellence

TEMPLE MANAGEMENT –
financial viability

Originally temples are financed by kings. After foreign
invasion, many temple lost their treasures.
 Presently, If pilgrims do not Patronise,
temple slowly decays and there are many temple in India
which are in ruins or very poor financial condition.
But Management or ownership CAN not change. A
comparison is drawn to Indian companies as management
does not change, even if the company becomes sick.
Recently bankruptcy is allowed in India companies.
Thus a company can be closed, unlike Temples.

© ABCD of Leadership

© copy Right . Source : from the forth coming book Titled "
Successful Management styles of India "

Economic Engineering Excellence

Temple Management Uniqueness - Multi chain of command (MCC)

- This is one common thing in India Management
- Single chain of command is prevalent in many small and even large enterprises,
- But few public domains are dotted with MCC (Multi Chain of Command)

   Eg. Indian Traffic and Indian Temples
- Enforcing discipline is difficult as communication to masses is poor leading to stampedes.

© copy Right   Source : from the forth coming book Titled "
Successful Management styles of India "

Temple Management – why Acceptable ?

- Indian tradition is not to question, but to obey.
- Mostly free and no compulsory contributions.
- Many charitable acts like poor feeding are associated with it.
- Resources are not the concern of general public
- No accountability
- Can participate if interested(voluntary work)
- No responsibility
- Engagement and entertainment as many temples are centres of arts.

© copy Right   Source : from the forth coming book Titled "
Successful Management styles of India "

Temple Management – Lessons

<u>Strengths :</u>

• Indian tradition suits Temple management .

• It is a top down management where all can also participate.

• Acceptability

• **<u>Weakness</u>** :

• Multi hierarchy

• Poor Communication

• Discipline

Temple Management tools adopted in Indian management

• Keep some aspects of management common so that all employees feel ownership eg. Social functions , festivals, charity and even arranging cricket and sports events etc.

• Maintain Inner democracy or Durbar , similar to Town Hall Meetings.

• Separate some activities for profit and some for social activities. Thus productivity is lost to celebrations but unity and comradeship is achieved. It is part of Employee engagement.

www.ingramcontent.com/pod-product-compliance
Lightning Source LLC
Chambersburg PA
CBHW021420210526
45463CB00001B/463